Walking by

FAITH

We love you
Mr. Fred!
Can't wait to see
you again; even if
we come across the
pond again!
Teddy & Kelly

Walking by FAITH

DR. TEDDY OTT

TATE PUBLISHING
AND **ENTERPRISES**, LLC

This book is designed to provide accurate and authoritative information with regard to the subject matter covered. This information is given with the understanding that neither the author nor Tate Publishing, LLC is engaged in rendering legal, professional advice. Since the details of your situation are fact dependent, you should additionally seek the services of a competent professional.

The opinions expressed by the author are not necessarily those of Tate Publishing, LLC.

Published by Tate Publishing & Enterprises, LLC
127 E. Trade Center Terrace | Mustang, Oklahoma 73064 USA
1.888.361.9473 | www.tatepublishing.com

Tate Publishing is committed to excellence in the publishing industry. The company reflects the philosophy established by the founders, based on Psalm 68:11,
"The Lord gave the word and great was the company of those who published it."

Book design copyright © 2016 by Tate Publishing, LLC. All rights reserved.
Cover design by Norlan Balazo
Interior design by Jomar Ouano

Published in the United States of America

ISBN: 978-1-68301-260-3
1. Religion / Christian Life / Devotional
2. Religion / Christian Life / Spiritual Growth
16.03.23

Contents

Foreword

My dad's faith in Jesus Christ began because God loved the world that He sent His only Son to save mankind (John 3:16) from the wages of their sins (Rom. 3:23). Therefore, Jesus died specifically for every individual on this earth. He does not wait for nor look for our meager attempts to save ourselves before He saves us. No, while we were still right in the middle of our sins, Christ died (Rom. 5:8) paid the whole price for our sins—death (Rom. 6:23).

At age six, my dad would believe in his heart and confessed with his mouth Jesus Christ as his Lord and Savior. He was baptized and began seeking to know and follow Jesus more closely. Over the past forty years, Daddy has spiritually matured in the faith. He believes that once we believe in our heart and confess with or mouth Jesus as Lord and Savior then we are called to follow Jesus as His disciple. Jesus commissions all those who believe to take up their cross and follow Him by going, teaching, and baptizing (Matthew 18:17-20; Luke 9:23; Romans

10:9). On top of that, God tells us to begin at home and everywhere we go and make disciples. We are then to keep going until Jesus reaches the whole world through us. He gives us the power to do so (Acts 1:8). My life is one step of faith at the time, denying myself and taking up my cross daily and following Jesus while allowing the Holy Spirit to make me look more like my Savior every day.

When I think of my daddy, Teddy Ott, I think of a man in pursuit of something greater than anything our eyes can see. He was not only my father, but also a mentor in my life. His faith in Jesus Christ began in the fall of 1974 at a Halloween carnival at Pinecrest Baptist Church in Thomasville, Alabama, where a Christian lady explained to him that we are all sinners and are in need of a savior. She went on to explain that because God so loved the world and everyone in it, He sent His only Son to save the world (John 3:16). This is where the pursuit of something great began in daddy's life.

He personally believes that he is a sinner and that Jesus Christ personally died for his sins. Daddy's testimony is that he deserves every dime of the death penalty required for his sin, and that it is a debt that he cannot pay. Therefore, because of God's great love for everyone, Jesus became the wage for him, and He paid his sin debt in full. His faith is in a Triune God: Father, Son, and Holy Spirit. His conviction is that the Word of God is inerrant, true, and complete, and that it is the guide we must use to live for Jesus. He wholeheartedly believes in the death, burial, resurrection, and the certain return of Jesus Christ for His own.

On April 28, 1979, God called daddy to be one of the select few to preach, and at age eleven, my dad would stand graveside and preach at his grandmother's funeral service. He did not surrender at that time nor did he understand the calling at that time, yet he knew that God was clearly calling him to be a pastor. It was not until 1990 at age twenty, while attending Howard Payne University, that he would clearly recognize God's call upon his life. Later that year, he would marry his life mate Kelly and would serve the next two years as youth minister in Seguin, Texas.

Their spiritual battle truly began as my mom, Kelly, told him, "You may be called into the ministry, but I am not. I am tired of being hurt." With that statement, daddy would resign as youth minister and leave the ministry for almost twelve years. Make no mistake, momma and daddy would grow to know that even when we are not in the pastoral ministry that we are still called to grow, serve, and minster. For my dad, this is the point where the pursuit of something greater would be put on hold for a season. After this season of patience, growth, and maturity, God had truly prepared my dad and my mom for a lifetime of ministry. The time of maturity had led my dad to wholeheartedly surrender to the call to ministry, and he was licensed into ministry in February 2002. Only two years later, he would be ordained as he was called to his first church in February 2004.

In January 2008, my dad completed a bachelor's degree in psychology and a religion degree from Liberty University and, in 2013, a master's degree in educational leadership from Lamar University. My dad has spent most of his ministry as a bivocational pastor. Therefore, he also taught school, coached, and drove a bus. At the completion of his master's degree, God led daddy to full-time work, and in February 2013, my dad became senior pastor of a church in Deep East Texas.

After becoming a full-time pastor, God led daddy to complete a PhD in Missions Evangelism and Church Growth. He finished this degree in December 2014. God has truly led my dad to become a committed lifetime learner for Christ's glory.

In January 2014, God told daddy that his ministry would soon take an even more dramatic turn, and in March 2014, his mom at age sixty-three died from a brain tumor, which was also on his daughter's wedding day. Little did Teddy know that he was also losing his health.

On June 8, 2014, my dad stood before the church he pastored and declared the need to fast and pray for twenty-one days. On Monday morning, he began fasting and praying. He would pray, "Lord, whatever it is that you want me to do, make it so clear that I can't back out." By Tuesday, daddy was sick, and his wife advised him to go see the doctor as he and his family were to go on a much-needed vacation the following Wednesday. After arriving at the doctor and after the doctor checked him over, the doctor left the room for a brief moment. He soon returned with these words: "Teddy, I have never told a patient this before, but I need you to separate your ministry from your health." To which my dad replied, "I can't do that." The doctor went on to say, "Teddy, if you don't, you won't have a ministry. Therefore, I need you out of the house that you are living in today and out of the area within thirty days because in the last twelve months, you have had pneumonia twice and been on steroids eight times."

Needless to say, my dad was shocked that he had been so busy with the ministry that he had not even remembered being sick so frequently. When he arrived home, he told his wife, Kelly, what the doctor said, and it was at that moment he was reminded what he had asked God earlier that morning. After continuing to fast and pray for the rest of the week, Sunday morning he would share with his church what the doctor had declared, and my dad resigned.

Boy, how his ministry had changed. Daddy had lost his mom, his health, and his church in just a short time, but despite all that, God had given my dad's writing ministry new heights. To this day, God continues to change my dad's life and the ministry to which He called him. Daddy continues to walk by faith, keeping his eyes solely on Jesus as the author and perfector of his faith.

Walking by faith is enduring; it is our allegiance, our loyalty to Jesus, our promise and sincerity to follow Him wherever He leads, and our determination keeps His commands, no matter what comes our way. Faith is trusting God for the outcome, no matter what the eyes see. We must place our hope for all things and in all areas in Jesus.

My dad has given me a true example of what it means to walk by faith. Does he always make the right decisions? No, he doesn't, but my dad is intent in his walk with the Lord.

Andrew Ott

Introduction

God led me to write this book as a devotional book, not to be mistaken for a book of devotions. This book is a forty-day, eight-chapter journey. Each of the eight chapters will contain a five-day devotional. In the chapters, one will encounter real-life stories from people who God is changing and molding us into His Son's image as they walk by faith.

This book was inspired by my mom. My mom faithfully walked with the Lord, and she has inspired so many to "walk by faith and not by sight." My mom was born in Selma, Alabama, on December 4, 1950. She was saved at an early age and walked faithfully with Jesus Christ for over fifty years. She loved to praise the Lord, and when she walked into a room, the room was immediately illuminated with the light of the Lord.

My mom married my dad on November 24, 1967. They were faithfully married for over forty-six years. My mom exuded faith in every area of her life, including her marriage. There was no doubt when examining her life that God was number one in every area. Did she have her flaws? Absolutely, but her love for Jesus and her love for others overshadowed them all. That is the key in life, to let our faith and wholehearted surrender to God overshadow wherever we have fallen short.

Make no mistake, my mom's life was not easy. Her mom and dad divorced before she was a teenager, she suffered severe cuts to her face as a child, she suffered from chronic allergies, and there was that uncertainty of the next meal when she was a child. The biggest challenge to her faith came in October 2010. That was the day that the doctors announced that she had a brain tumor nicknamed "The Death Sentence." This would shake our world, but not my mom's faith. Phrases like, "I walk by faith and not by sight," "By His stripes I am healed," and "No worries, God is in control" would ring out consistently in the days that followed. The doctor announced to the family that she had glioblastoma multiforme, and she had about six months to one year to live if they removed the tumor, and her reply was, "No worries, God is in control."

Dr. Chow removed the first tumor. That morning we received calls from people interceding in prayer. One call from her chiropractor stated that they had a prayer chain of over four hundred going. Needless to say, we were overwhelmed with support. About four hours later, Dr. Chow returned to tell us that he had gotten all the tumor that he could, and he felt that since he had taken so much of her brain that she would lose her speech as well as her long-term memory. Much to his surprise as he walked to the back, my mom told him that "God was funny." Momma never lost any memory or her sight.

A few months later she had to go to the hospital as she was going downhill quickly. The doctor told us that day that the tumor had returned with a vengeance. It was double the size, and this time wreaking havoc on her brain stem. Battling pneumonia and various other complications, we eventually took her home with the doctors giving her about two weeks to live. A few days later, we took her to a hospice house where we found out that she had two days to live. My mom's faith in the absolute sovereignty of God would take her out of hospice that second day and make her cancer free/tumor free. My mom was a lady who truly walked by faith.

This book is devoted to leading every reader to truly walk by faith. We must never forget the blessings that are found in the Rewarder, Jesus, as we diligently seek Him as we walk by faith.

Faith Is a Life-Changing Relationship

Our faith is Christ can be described as a life-changing relationship. Knowing who Jesus is, what He did for us, and what He will do should cause an eternity of change in our lives. Anything less seeks to devalue the price Jesus paid for each of us. We must not devalue the price that Jesus paid. He died for the sins of all mankind individually. Somehow when we blanket what He did with the conclusion that He died for everyone at one time, we seem to water down what Jesus actually did for us individually. He died for our sins individually. He did not corporately save us, but He saved us individually. Therefore, walking by faith begins with a personal relationship with Jesus, and not a corporate one. As a result, we have individual responsibilities as a corporate body of believers. We must individually walk with Jesus daily.

What does a personal relationship with Jesus Christ look like? It looks like total surrender. When we personally understand that we are a sinner for whom Christ died then we will surrender to the truth that we earned every dime of that debt. We believe that death is and remains a penalty that we individually owe but cannot pay. Therefore, because of His great love for us, as individuals, Jesus paid the price for us, and He paid it completely. We believe that because of each individual's sin that there was a great chasm between us and God, but that Jesus—as the only way to the Father, the Truth, and the Life—has bridged the way for our personal restoration. We believe in a Triune God: Father, Son, and Holy Spirit. We believe that the Word of God is inerrant, true, complete, and that it is the guide to living our life for Jesus. We believe wholeheartedly in the death, burial, resurrection, and the certain return of Jesus Christ for His own. We believe that we are being sanctified and changed to look more like Jesus by the Holy Spirit so that we can live in the abundant life that Jesus promised as we take up our cross daily and follow Him (2 Cor. 3:18, Luke 9:23).

So what does a changed life look like? Before answering this question directly, we must recognize the truth that the basic work of every Christian life is to preach the gospel of Jesus Christ, in the power of the Holy Spirit, see people converted, changed, and then grow to maturity in the gospel. That is ministry. We do so corporately and individually. So what began personally is to be personally lived out corporately. Jesus describes this as the work of planting, watering, fertilizing, and tending the vine. Just as some sort of framework is needed to help a vine grow, we need the support system that God put in place to grow and mature us in the faith. Jesus said,

> I am the true vine, and my Father is the vinedresser. Every branch in me that does not bear fruit he takes away, and every branch that does bear fruit he prunes, that it may bear more fruit. Already you are clean because of the word that I have spoken to you. Abide in me, and I in you. As the branch cannot bear fruit by itself, unless it abides in the vine, neither can you, unless you abide in me. I am the vine; you are the branches. Whoever abides in me and I in him, he it is that bears much fruit, for apart from me you can do nothing. If anyone does not abide in me he is thrown away like a branch and withers; and the branches are gathered, thrown into the fire, and burned. If you abide in me, and my words abide in you, ask whatever you wish, and it will be done for you. By this my Father is glorified, that you bear much fruit and so prove to be my disciples. As the Father has loved me, so have I loved you. Abide in my love. If you keep my commandments, you will abide in my love, just as I have kept my Father's commandments and abide in his love. These things I have spoken to you, that my joy may be in you, and that your joy may be full. (John 15:1–11, ESV)

Therefore we abide in the vine (Jesus) as the Holy Spirit shapes us into the image of Christ, does the work of Christ through us, and guides us, but we must have systems and supports that lead us to a greater surrender to God and His work. We must beware that the vinedresser (the Father) will even prune us to make us grow.

We grow as we go!

> And Jesus came up and spoke to them saying, "All authority has been given to Me in heaven and on earth." And He said to them, "Go into all the world and preach the gospel to all creation... and make disciples of all the nations, baptizing them in the name of the Father and the Son and the Holy Spirit, teaching them to observe all that I have commanded you: He who has believed and has been baptized shall be saved; but He who has disbelieved shall be condemned. Thus it is written, that the Christ should suffer and rise again from the dead the third day; and that repentance for the forgiveness of sins should be proclaimed in His name to all the nations, beginning from Jerusalem." (Matt. 28:18–20, ESV)

The main verb here is *go*, meaning "wherever you go" followed closely by the verb *make*, meaning "I am to do the work of actively sharing the gospel message of Christ everywhere I go, and then make them disciples. I am to make disciples by teaching everyone who is saved to obey Jesus's every command." In other words, we are to mature into disciples and then disciple makers. Every disciple will follow and obey the Word of God. Therefore, disciples must study and obey God's word, which will lead them to follow closely behind Jesus Christ.

- A disciple "is willing to deny self, take up a cross daily, and follow Him" (Luke 9:23–25).
- A disciple "puts Christ before self, family, and possessions" (Luke 14:25–35)
- A disciple "is committed to Christ's teachings." This speaks to His Word (John 8:31).
- A disciple "is committed to world evangelism" (Matt. 9:36–38).
- A disciple "loves others as Christ loves" (John 13:34–35).
- A disciple "abides in Christ, is obedient, bears fruit, glorifies God, has joy and loves the brethren" (John 15:7–17)

So a changed life will mature, and as it does, it will conclude that it is not our life, but instead a life that belongs to Christ.

> For you were bought at a price; therefore glorify God in your body and in your spirit, which are God's. (1 Cor. 6:20)

John 3:30 says, "He must increase, but I must decrease."

Fortunately for us, we don't have to rely on "guesses" or "hunches" when we make choices in life. We must ask ourselves, "Are you going to live your life God's Way or your way?"

There is a Hebrew word *dabaq* (dah-bach) or (dah-bock). It means "passionately fixing our heart on Him." It means to be loyal no matter what! *Dabaq* is used in the following verses:

> My heart is fixed, O God, my heart is fixed: I will sing and give praise. Psalm 57:7

> My soul follows hard after thee: thy right hand holds me. Psalm 63:8

In other words, we are to cling to Him, holding on to God for dear life! It is the heart that says, "I don't want to leave!" "I can't leave!" Or "How dare I leave!"

There is an excellent biblical example of one person who made His choice that provides for us the best example of fixing our mind and heart on living life God's Way. That example is Jesus Christ Himself. Jesus was put to the test to see if He would make a deal with the devil at the beginning of His earthly ministry. This was before Jesus performed any miracle, offered any public teaching, or preached any sermon. Jesus had gone into the wilderness to demonstrate to us his commitment to the Father's will.

Matthew 4:1–3 tells the story: "Then Jesus was led up by the Spirit into the wilderness to be tempted by the devil. And when He had fasted forty days and forty nights, afterward He was hungry. Now when the tempter came to Him, he said, 'If You are the Son of God, command that these stones become bread.'

Jesus had made His choice. He said, "I am going to the cross!" Satan tried to tempt Jesus to compromise by saying, "Come on, you know that your choice isn't satisfying you at this moment! You're hungry, and it is not going to hurt anything to put some food in your stomach, is it? So look here, I have a better offer for you: forget what God the Father said [to fast and pray] and turn these stones into bread! Just think about yourself and forget about all the souls for now. You can worry about those later and satisfy your hunger."

Isn't it like Satan to try to get us to put off what God is clearly telling us to do just for immediate personal gratification? Not Jesus. He quickly replied, "No way!" Matthew 4:4 says it this way: "But He answered and said, 'It is written, "Man shall not live by bread alone, but by every word that proceeds from the mouth of God."'"

Some readers are still wondering, what's wrong with eating? Especially eating when you are hungry. Well, nothing, unless God tells us not to, but when He tells us not to do something, it immediately becomes an obedience issue. We must always keep in mind that disobedience to God is the very definition of sin.

So one evidence of a changed life is the ability to say no to selfish desires and live life God's Way.

The evidence a changed life and life walking with God is one that says, "It is not my time, it is His!" When you hear words like "Give God your time," we think things like "We have to go to church more frequently or get more involved in more church-sponsored activities," but there is so much more to giving God our time. It is much more than accumulating more hours inside a church building. We are to give God all of our time all the time and every single moment of our existence. When Jesus says, "As you go" (Matt. 28:18), He is telling us that we should commune with God and spend time with Him everywhere we go. In other words, we should have a "God moment" every moment of our life—from the beginning of our day, throughout our day, and at the end of our day. It should be time well spent with God.

Martin Luther, the great Protestant reformer of the mid-1500s, in response to being informed of his schedule of events and responsibilities one day, said this: "I have so much to do today that I should spend the first three hours in prayer." He knew that he had so much to accomplish that he couldn't possibly be successful on his own, so it must be bathed in prayer. Isn't that the opposite of how we view a busy day? We often respond like, "Sorry, God, I don't have time for this morning, but I'll catch you tomorrow morning." And guess what, we never catch up with Him.

Remember this principle: ""The busier we get the more time we must spend with the One who created and sustains the day." Psalm 1:1–3 puts it this way:

> Blessed is the man, Who walks not in the counsel of the ungodly, Nor stands in the path of sinners, Nor sits in the seat of the scornful; But his delight is in the law of the LORD, And in His law he meditates day and night. He shall be like a tree, Planted by the rivers of water, That brings forth its fruit in its season, Whose leaf also shall not wither; And whatever he does shall prosper. (Ps. 1:1–3)

First Thessalonians 5:17 sums up how in three words: "Pray without ceasing." Everywhere we go, we are to think about God, talk to God, and meditate on His greatness. All that we do and say should reflect time with God. Titus 2:1–8 says,

> But as for you, speak the things which are proper for sound doctrine: that the older men be sober, reverent, temperate, sound in faith, in love, in patience; the older women likewise, that they be reverent in behavior, not slanderers, not given to much wine, teachers of good things that they admonish the young women to love their husbands, to love their children, to be discreet, chaste, homemakers, good, obedient to their own husbands, that the word of God may not be blasphemed. Likewise, exhort the young men to be sober-minded, in all things showing

yourself to be a pattern of good works; in doctrine showing integrity, reverence, incorruptibility, sound speech that cannot be condemned, that one who is an opponent may be ashamed, having nothing evil to say of you.

First Peter 3:15 says, "But sanctify the Lord God in your hearts, and always be ready to give a defense to everyone who asks you a reason for the hope that is in you, with meekness and fear." This point is further supported by 2 Timothy 4:2: "Preach the word! Be ready in season and out of season. Convince, rebuke, exhort, with all longsuffering and teaching." Be ready "any time."

Time with God includes time with family, time with others, and time with the church. Family, others, and the church are priorities that come right after putting God first, which actually means our time with all of these should always be an encounter with God. For example, the church is one large God-ordained support system to support our spiritual life, at times your physical life, and even your social life. To make God a priority is to schedule other events around church, and not church around other events. In other words, we need to give God our "schedule." God ordained the family, and He ordained the church. So He wants our time with Him to be time with family. We must be clear on the fact that our family includes our spiritual family. Spending time with fellow believers, worshiping with them, studying God's word with them, and conversing with them about spiritual things can really refuel us and energize us to make it through our week. But giving God our time at church does not simply mean that we attend. The goal is to go, grow, and sow. God is a worthy recipient of our time.

We will know that we are walking with God when we say with our treasure, "It's not my treasure, it's His!" We must be ready at all times to follow God's Way with the resources that He has placed in our care. We are to be good stewards of those resources.

On Sunday evening, July 6, 2003, Dr. Jerry Falwell preached a sermon entitled "Stewardship Is a Spiritual Matter," and I'd like to echo some familiar truths regarding giving God our treasure.

1. We should give out of conviction.
   A conviction that our giving should be based on scripture. We should consider making our life one long gift to others. All that we have is on loan anyway. Jerry Falwell said, "All that lasts is what you pass on." Proverbs 3:9 says, "Honor the LORD with your possessions, and with the first fruits of all your increase; So your barns will be filled with plenty, And your vats will overflow with new wine."

2. We should give with clarity.
   The Bible is clear. It is not confusing regarding the issue of giving. We should know why we give to

God and know its purpose. In 2 Corinthians 11:3, Paul says, "But I fear, lest somehow, as the serpent deceived Eve by his craftiness, so your minds may be corrupted from the simplicity that is in Christ." There is a simplicity that is in Christ that provides an elementary infrastructure for all areas of obedient living and giving that includes the giving of our time, talents, treasures, temple, and testimony. The first tenth of all our increase belongs to God. The first tenth is to be given on the first day of the week, Sunday. First Corinthians 16:2 says, "On the first day of the week let each one of you lay something aside, storing up as he may prosper, that there be no collections when I come."

3. We should give out concern for the needy.
   Even if it takes a level of sacrifice to meet their needs, we give what they need. Scripture says that sacrificial giving is a lifestyle. The churches of Macedonia were sacrificial givers, and that is what God wants us to be. Second Corinthians 8:1–2 says, "Moreover, brethren, we make known to you the grace of God bestowed on the churches of Macedonia: that in a great trial of affliction the abundance of their joy and their deep poverty abounded in the riches of their liberality."

4. We should give to our church.

   The first tenth is to be given in the first house, God's church. Malachi 3:10 says, "Bring all the tithes into the storehouse, That there may be food in My house, And try Me now in this," Says the Lord of hosts, "If I will not open for you the windows of heaven And pour out for you such blessing That there will not be room enough to receive it."

   God has given us the trust to be good stewards of His resources.

5. We should give out of compassion for the lost.

   Second Corinthians 8:3–5 says, "For I bear witness that according to their ability, yes, and beyond their ability, they were freely willing, imploring us with much urgency that we would receive the gift and the fellowship of the ministering to the saints. And not only as we had hoped, but they first gave themselves to the Lord, and then to us by the will of God."

   Because Jesus gave His all for us, we must give our all for Him!

   The evidence a changed life and life walking with God is one that says, "It's not my Temple…it's His." I am saying that God calls for us to offer our hearts, lives, and bodies to be a pure sacrifice, similar to what the physical Jewish temple was utilized for. Paul, in his statements to the religious debaters, made this statement about how God dwells in our hearts—our spiritual temples—if we are believers in Jesus Christ.

Acts 17:24–28 (NKJV) reminds us that

> God, who made the world and everything in it, since He is Lord of heaven and earth, does not dwell in temples made with hands. Nor is He worshiped with men's hands, as though He needed anything, since He gives to all life, breath, and all things. And He has made from one blood every nation of men to dwell on all the face of the earth, and has determined their pre-appointed times and the boundaries of their dwellings, so that they should seek the Lord, in the hope that they might grope for Him and find Him, though He is not far from each one of us; for in Him we live and move and have our being.

The same text according to the NLT translations says,

> He is the God who made the world and everything in it. Since he is Lord of heaven and earth, he doesn't live in man-made temples, and human hands can't serve his needs—for he has no needs. He himself gives life and breath to everything, and he satisfies every need. From one man he created all the nations through-

out the whole earth. He decided beforehand when they should rise and fall, and he determined their boundaries. His purpose was for the nations to seek after God and perhaps feel their way toward him and find him—though he is not far from any one of us. For in him we live and move and exist.

When we compare the way people prepared to come to the physical temple for worship to the way we need to prepare our own temples to be presented to God in worship, God desires our spiritual temples to be arranged with five spiritual conditions:

a. Our temples must be temples of *worship*!

When a person would approach the temple in biblical times, they had to be prepared to worship. The way we approach the temple paints a clear picture as to whether or not we are walking by faith. Jeremiah 26:2 states, "Thus says the LORD: Stand in the court of the Lord's house, and speak to all the cities of Judah that come to worship in the house of the LORD, all the words that I command you to speak to them; do not hold back a word."

The moment that Jesus ascended back into heaven after rising from the dead, notice where the disciples went and what they did. Luke 24:50–53 says,

And He led them out as far as Bethany, and He lifted up His hands and blessed them. Now it came to pass, while He blessed them, that He was parted from them and carried up into heaven. And they worshiped Him, and returned to Jerusalem with great joy, and were continually in the temple praising and blessing God.

In a similar manner, if we belong to Christ and we claim to be walking by faith, then our temples must be a constant residence of praise and worship for God. How do you know if we have given our temple to God? Simply ask yourself, "Is my heart a heart that exudes praise and worship for the Lord?" The physical temple of the Bible was made for worship, and anyone who came to that temple should expect worship to be occurring. Likewise, if God examines our heart, He should expect for worship to be occurring there! It is a sobering yet true reality: an absence of worship in the temple is to fear the absence of God in the temple! Is your temple yielded to God? Is it a temple of praise and worship? Because "it's not our temple...it's His!"

b. Our temples should be temples of humility.
It follows logically that as a result of praising God and standing in His greatness and worshiping Him,

it will indeed humble us. When you would approach the temple in biblical times, you had to approach the temple reverently. What is interesting about the actual stairway that led up to the temple is that the steps are different sizes and widths (you can actually walk up this staircase today). Some believe that the staircase was built this way so that those coming up to God in worship could not rush right up to God in a hasty, disrespectful manner so as to be disrespectful to God. The varying steps and widths would make you have to always keep your head down in humility so as to make sure you were approaching God in a humble disposition.

When we cultivate the temple within us, we need to do so knowing that we can't do it on our own. In fact, we were never meant to even attempt this task on our own. It is God's power working through us that allows us to live and move and be all that God intends. Second Corinthians 4:7 says, "But we have this treasure in earthen vessels, that the excellence of the power may be of God and not of us." And Paul in Galatians 2:20 declares, "I have been crucified with Christ; it is no longer I who live, but Christ lives in me; and the life which I now live in the flesh I live by faith in the Son of God, who loved me and gave Himself for me."

c. Our temples must be pure.

God will at times break us in order to purify us. When people would approach the temple in biblical times, they did so only after being fully cleansed. In fact, prior to stepping into the temple to worship, one had to wash their entire body in a *mikvah* (*mick*-vah). A *mikvah* was kind of like our baptismal tanks today. They were located near the entrance of the temple. They would dunk themselves symbolically, much like taking a shower today. They did so as to say to the Lord, "My body is clean and so is my heart, now I am ready to worship." Believers in Jesus Christ are supposed do so with a pure, repentant heart that is fully surrendered to Jesus and therefore holy before Him.

Psalm 24:3–4 says, "Who may ascend into the hill of the LORD? Or who may stand in His holy place? He who has clean hands and a pure heart, who has not lifted up his soul to an idol, nor sworn deceitfully." And 2 Corinthians 6:14–20 says,

> Do not be unequally yoked together with unbelievers. For what fellowship has righteousness with lawlessness? And what communion has light with darkness? And what accord has Christ with Belial? Or what part has a believer with an unbeliever? And what agreement has the temple of God with idols? For you are the

temple of the living God. As God has said: "I will dwell in them and walk among them. I will be their God, and they shall be My people." Therefore "Come out from among them and be separate, says the Lord. Do not touch what is unclean, and I will receive you. I will be a Father to you, and you shall be My sons and daughters," says the LORD Almighty.

One word of caution at this point: when the temple is being used for impure purposes, then God will cleanse it! Remember Mark 11:15–17 where it says,

> So they came to Jerusalem. Then Jesus went into the temple and began to drive out those who bought and sold in the temple, and over-turned the tables of the money changers and the seats of those who sold doves. And He would not allow anyone to carry wares through the temple. Then He taught, saying to them, "Is it not written, 'My house shall be called a house of prayer for all nations'? But you have made it a 'den of thieves.'"

d. Our temples must be guarded.

As one approached the temple in biblical times, they would immediately notice the very obvious presence of temple guards posted at strategic positions. This was especially true during busy times. The guards were not only for physical protection, but for the purpose of keeping order and to prevent anything unclean or unacceptable from entering into the temple, thereby hindering worship. In a similar manner, we too need a guarded temple. Second Corinthians 10:4–6 explains exactly how we are to protect our temple from sin by pursuing holiness and allowing it to channel all our energy toward obedience. The scripture says,

> For the weapons of our warfare are not carnal but mighty in God for pulling down strongholds, casting down arguments and every high thing that exalts itself against the knowledge of God, bringing every thought into captivity to the obedience of Christ, and being ready to punish all disobedience when your obedience is fulfilled. (2 Cor. 10:4–6)

e. Our temples must be broken.
    We have to get to the point in our lives as believers that we so moved with compassion that our hearts literally broke or were burdened to see everyone come to the saving knowledge of Jesus Christ. Our hearts must actually ache or break over sin in our own life and the lives of others. Therefore, we have a longing desire for everyone we meet to love God and to honor God through their lives. Our heart's passion should fully reflect God's passion.

First Timothy 2:4 says we must be those "who desire all men to be saved and to come to the knowledge of the truth." A person truly walking by faith knows that just as God desires us to broken over sin and to see people break free from the bonds of sin, He also desires to repair every broken temple.

The truth is our temples have become tarnished and vandalized by the scars of unrepentant sin. John 8:3–11 says,

> Then the scribes and Pharisees brought to Him a woman caught in adultery. And when they had set her in the midst, they said to Him, "Teacher, this woman was caught in adultery, in the very act. Now Moses, in the law, commanded us that such should be stoned. But what do You say?" This they said, testing Him, that they might have something of which to accuse Him. But Jesus stooped down and wrote on the ground with His finger, as though He did not hear. So when they continued asking Him, He raised Himself up and said to them, "He who is without sin among you, let him throw a stone at her first." And again He stooped down and wrote on the ground. Then those who heard it, being convicted by their conscience, went out one by one, beginning with the oldest even to the last. And Jesus was left alone, and the woman standing in the

midst. When Jesus had raised Himself up and saw no one but the woman, He said to her, "Woman, where are those accusers of yours? Has no one condemned you?" She said, "No one, Lord." And Jesus said to her, "Neither do I condemn you; go and sin no more."

The same love that builds up our temple, cleanses our temple, and guards our temple is the same love that restores our temple. The keys to our temple are meant for Jesus Christ alone.

The evidence a changed life and life walking with God is one that says, "It's not my talent, it's His!" Talent alone can never bring us any eternal reward, and we can never make an eternal impact on our own. First Peter 4:10–11 says,

> As each one has received a gift, minister it to one another, as good stewards of the manifold grace of God. If anyone speaks, let him speak as the oracles of God. If anyone ministers, let him do it as with the ability which God supplies, that in all things God may be glorified through Jesus Christ, to whom belong the glory and the dominion forever and ever. Amen.

We must use our talents solely to minister to God and serve others, even when we feel we have no talent. There is no better passage that depicts the picture of how inadequate and feeble our talents are apart from God's power than the picture of Moses in Exodus 3 and 4. These chapters describe a conversation that God had through a burning bush to Moses. God was telling Moses that he was to go back to Egypt and tell Pharaoh to free God's people from slavery.

We are going to look at a picture where God is telling this normal human being (Moses) right in the middle of all his excuses, his reasons, and his rational as to why God can't use him. "I am going use you!" God is telling Moses that He is not looking for Moses's ability, but instead God was looking for his availability.

Jesus is saying to us today, "Apart from me, you can do nothing, but with me, all things are possible," just as Jesus said to the disciples in Matthew 19:26. This is great encouragement; when we relinquish our goals, our lives, our finances, and our all over to Him and do all we do for His glory, then great things will be done. That is walking by faith.

When we are walking by faith, we live to make an eternal God-glorifying difference in the world we live in as we totally rely on the Lord to empower us. If we don't, then our efforts are fleeting and futile. God's promise is that He will always sustain us when we desire to live for His glory. When we do, then He will extract out of us our God-given abilities and impact the world for His glory.

There are four frequent excuses and responses from God for not giving and using our talents wholeheartedly for the Lord.

1. We feel unworthy!

   Exodus 3:10–11 says, "'Come now, therefore, and I will send you to Pharaoh that you may bring My people, the children of Israel, out of Egypt.' But Moses said to God, 'Who am I that I should go to Pharaoh, and that I should bring the children of Israel out of Egypt?'"

   In other words, Moses was saying, "Me, I am not the one, God! Do you not know what I've done? I used to be the one to oversee the slaves while I was considered a son of Pharaoh! I brought about hardships upon them, I killed a man and had to flee, I'm not worthy to be used in this capacity!"

   God's Response: "I will be with you!" Exodus 3:12 says, "So He said, 'I will certainly be with you. And this shall be a sign to you that I have sent you: When you have brought the people out of Egypt, you shall serve God on this mountain.'"

2. We think that no one will believe us!

   Exodus 4:1 states, "Then Moses answered and said, 'But suppose they will not believe me or listen to my voice; suppose they say, "The LORD has not appeared to you."'"

   God's Response: "You just leave it up to me for the power of the message; you just deliver it!"

So the LORD said to him, "What is that in your hand?" He said, "A rod." And He said, "Cast it on the ground." So he cast it on the ground, and it became a serpent; and Moses fled from it. Then the LORD said to Moses, "Reach out your hand and take it by the tail" (and he reached out his hand and caught it, and it became a rod in his hand), "that they may believe that the LORD God of their fathers, the God of Abraham, the God of Isaac, and the God of Jacob, has appeared to you." (Exod. 4:2–5)

3. We are afraid to speak in front of others.
    Exodus 4:10 says, "Then Moses said to the LORD, 'O my Lord, I am not eloquent, neither before nor since You have spoken to Your servant; but I am slow of speech and slow of tongue.'"

    God's Response: "I am not relying on your ability to speak, but instead I want you to rely on My strength and ability!"

    So the Lord said to him, "Who has made man's mouth? Or who makes the mute, the deaf, the seeing, or the blind? Have not I, the Lord? Now therefore, go, and I will be with your mouth and teach you what you shall say." (Exod. 4:11–12)

4. We feel that unable.

Exodus 4:13 says, "But he said, 'O my Lord, please send by the hand of whomever else You may send.'"

Remember, this is after God had reassured Moses over and over again not to feel inadequate, but that God Himself was with him every step of the way. Isn't it great that God will prove His faithfulness to us over and over? God is patient, and He is long-suffering. He is always willing to give us a little more time to comprehend what He is teaching us. God will always take care of our every need. He will always take our abilities as we give wholly to Him, and he will give us power, endurance, the right words, and everything else that we need to do all that He asks.

What happens when we remain in our excuses instead of walking by faith? Exodus 4:14–16 says,

> So the anger of the LORD was kindled against Moses, and He said: "Is not Aaron the Levite your brother? I know that he can speak well. And look, he is also coming out to meet you. When he sees you, he will be glad in his heart. Now you shall speak to him and put the words in his mouth. And I will be with your mouth and with his mouth, and I will teach you what you shall do. So he shall be your spokesman to the people. And he himself shall be as a mouth for you, and you shall be to him as God."

God got mad about Moses's excuses, but God would still use him and bless him.

It is not our talent, abilities, or strengths that we rely on to build a great life, church, ministry, or family. It is all about our ability to totally rely on what God can do through our talents, strengths, and abilities! A child of God who is walking by faith realizes that it is not our life, our time, our treasure, our temple, our testimony, our talent, but instead they all belong to God. We must learn to choose God's Way in every decision to how we use our life, time, treasure, temple, testimony, and talent. When we do, then we will be walking by faith.

Day 1

Walking in Confident Assurance

Now faith is the assurance of things hoped for, the conviction of things not seen. For by it the people of old received their commendation. By faith we understand that the universe was created by the word of God, so that what is seen was not made out of things that are visible.

—Hebrews 11:1–3 (ESV)

There are three biblical phrases that often come to mind as I think of my mom. They are the following: "No worries, God is in control," "By His stripes I am healed," and the one that led me to the devotional series this week, "I walk by faith and not by sight." As children of God, we know that "for by grace we have been saved through faith. And this is not our own doing; it is the gift of God." So the grace of God channeled into our lives through our faith in Jesus Christ is how we are saved, but what is faith? The word *faith* here may also be translated as "belief or trust."

Dr. Adrian Rogers once said, "Faith first involves an agreement. We mentally agree that something is true in our heart. Then, we consciously say our heartfelt amen to what God has said and we are persuaded, but that agreement is not yet faith. Our agreement then turns into an attitude. The attitude that comes out of that agreement is confidence or trust. So we first believe it to be true and then because we believe it to be true we put confidence and trust in it and it's not quite faith yet, but it is very close now. But because we believe it to be true and it has a made its place in our heart we then act on it and it becomes faith. Agreement plus attitude plus action is true bible faith."

Faith is the confident assurance that what God tells us has happened absolutely happened and is true, and what God says will happen is going to happen without a shadow of a doubt. Faith is not a feeling or emotion. It is the very foundation of our relationship with God. Faith is what Jesus is building the church upon. Faith is surety that does not rest on logical proof or material evidence, but is a complete understanding that God did everything described in His word and will do everything He has promised. Faith is not something we have as much as the way we live.

Hebrews 11:1–3 puts a big concept in a few simple words: "Now faith is being sure of what we hope for and certain of what we do not see."

A. W. Tozer said, "Faith is seeing the invisible, but not the nonexistent." Some people think faith is believing in something that is not actually there, but that is not true. Faith is believing wholeheartedly in the one true God. Real faith or biblical faith believes that when God tells us something, it is done and we can take it to the bank, so to speak. It does not matter whether we can see it happening or not; we know with all our heart that it will happen. Faith means that we keep our eyes on God, who controls all circumstances, and not on the circumstances themselves. Second Corinthians 5:7 puts it this way: we live by faith, not by sight.

> Lord, help us to clearly walk by faith and not by sight. And as we walk by faith, help us to honor you by walking uprightly in Your word, staying close by Your side, and may we look for You in every situation and circumstance because we wholeheartedly know that You are there with us. Lord, may we truly walk by faith today. Amen.

Day 2
What Walking by Faith Is Not!

For by grace you have been saved through faith.
And this is not your own doing; it is the gift of
God, not a result of works,
so that no one may boast.

—Ephesians 2:8–9 (esv)

For some people, walking by faith sounds simple enough, but faith is not something we can produce on our own. *"It is not your own doing so that no one may boast."* Faith is not manufactured. "Faith comes from hearing, and hearing through the word of Christ" (Rom. 10:17, NLT). Faith is a by-product of the gospel message. Faith is produced as we meditate upon, study, and obey the word of God.

For some reason, many of us get all kinds of misconceptions about what faith is, and so let's take a few minutes to look at what biblical faith is *not*. I have always found that when our misconceptions are wiped away, this allows room for the truth to shine through.

Faith is not sight. In fact, faith is not seeing clearly, but instead trusting completely. "By faith we understand that the universe was formed at God's command, so that what is seen was not made out of what was visible" (Heb. 11:3). God never intended us to construct our own faith based on our situations, circumstances, or simply what we can see. No, the Christian faith is not compatible with logic and reason. It is based on something more concrete. It is based on truth. "Jesus is the way the Truth and the life" (John 14:6). Faith is based on historical evidence. Faith is supported by biblical record, by personal testimony, and by our own experiences.

D. L. Moody said, "I prayed for faith and thought that some day it would come down and strike me like lightning. But, faith didn't seem to come. One day I read in Romans, 'Faith comes by hearing and hearing by the word of God,' and up to this time I had closed my Bible and prayed for faith. Now I opened my Bible and began to study, and my faith has been growing ever since." Faith comes from a being deeply rooted in the Word of God.

Another misconception about faith is that faith is getting God to do anything we want.

Faith is not the ability to get what we want. Some Christians think that faith is a kind of magic or like fairy dust. We think a little sprinkle is all you need, so we name it and claim it, or we blab it and grab it, and *poof*, it magically appears, but that kind of faith won't outlast our first major disappointment. When we see faith this way, the first time a loved one is not healed, a promotion doesn't come through, or unforeseen tragedy strikes someone we love, then this pseudofaith will disappear as quickly as it appeared. Biblical faith does not believe that God will do what we say, but instead, biblical faith knows that God will do what *He* says, and by faith, we rest on the promises of God, no matter what happens.

Faith is not *a simple process of following the rules.* We must never make faith about being good enough or following the rules. Biblical faith is a personal relationship with God. In the Old Testament, God is often referred to as the God of Abraham, Isaac, and Jacob. If you think about it, this makes sense. Suppose you wanted to tell someone who Teddy Ott is. Well, you could give my SS number, my DL number, or my bank account number. You might tell them my address, age, height, weight, my physical structure, or my occupation. But if you really wanted someone to know *who* I am, you could say, "Teddy is Andrew and Marybeth's daddy, he is a child of God, the son of Terry and Rosemary, and the husband of Kelly." If you want to know what someone is like, look at their personal relationships and the people they spend most of their time with, the ones that they care about most, and then look at the people who care about them most to get a clear picture. If you want to know who God is, look at Him personally; look at the people He cares for and the people who care about Him.

> Lord, help us to clearly walk by faith as we understand what faith is not. Lord, we ask that faith be manifest in our life as we are firmly planted in Your Word. Lord, help us to walk by faith and not by sight. Amen.

Day 3

Walking by Faith Takes Courage

So we are always of good courage. We know that while we are at home in the body we are away from the Lord, for we walk by faith, not by sight.

—2 Corinthians 5:6–7

Now that we have discussed what faith is not, let's glean from God's Word a clear picture of faith. The New Testament describes faith in four facets.

> Now faith is the assurance of things hoped for, the conviction [confidence] of things not seen. For by it the people of old received their commendation. By faith we understand that the universe was created by the word of God, so that what is seen was not made out of things that are visible. (Heb. 11:1–3, ESV)

Faith is assurance. The first facet of faith is the assurance in/of the Savior. In other words, we know that we know that Jesus, God incarnate, came from heaven to save us, and while we were still in the middle of our sin, He died on the cross for us. Jesus did not stop there, but He then defeated the grave (death) once and for all for us (which was the penalty of our sin), and He rose from the dead, giving us eternal life. I praise God that Jesus was not done when He rose from the dead either, but instead He ascended to the

Father, and today with the assurance of Jesus's return for His own, we wait for Him.

So faith is confident assurance in the Savior that we are saved. We confidently proclaim that we have a saving faith. A saving faith is where our eternal journey begins. It all begins with believing, but once we believe, faith will not let us rest in our salvation, but faith demands that we follow Jesus. Therefore, we are to put feet to our faith. That is what it means to walk by faith and not by sight. Faith becomes the steering wheel of our life. It is what drives us to dare to go wherever God leads. It is what leads us to take the next step when we cannot see the path clearly, but we can see Jesus, so we keep moving toward Him. That is why in James 2:14–17, James says, "What does it profit, my brethren, if someone says he has faith but does not have works? Can faith save him? If a brother or sister is naked and destitute of daily food, and one of you says to them, 'Depart in peace, be warmed and filled,' but you do not give them the things which are needed for the body, what does it profit? Thus also faith by itself, if it does not have works, is dead." Faith always produces good fruit (works).

Faith is confidence. We are to continuously trust in God's promises. We must be confident that whatever our Father has promised us, it's ours the very moment He made the promise. That is the confidence that we have. We are confident that He will never leave us nor forsake us, but we are confident that He will provide everything that we will ever need, we are confident in His protection, we are confident in His love, His guidance, His strength, and the list could go on. Our confidence must always rest in God and God alone. We can count on His every Word right now. We are not waiting on His promises, but instead His promises are always waiting us to confidently take hold of them. That is faith.

Faith is understanding. Psalm 119:130 (NAS) says, "The opening of thy words giveth light; It giveth understanding unto the simple." Faith is understanding that God's every word is true and that Jesus is the way, the truth, and the life and the only way to the Father. Faith is understanding that Jesus is everything, He is all that we need, and that God has provided everything that we need to live the godly life that He calls us to. Faith is understanding that nothing can pluck us out of God's mighty hand, and nothing can separates us from the love of Jesus.

> Who shall separate us from the love of Christ? shall tribulation, or distress, or persecution, or famine, or nakedness, or peril, or sword? As it is written, For thy sake we are killed all the day long; we are accounted as sheep for the slaughter. Nay, in all these things we are more than conquerors through him that loved us. (Rom. 8:35–37)

Faith understands that we are more than conquerors in Christ Jesus. Faith in Jesus always leads us to complete assurance, confidence, and understanding. Do you have the courage to walk by faith today? We must remember faith never falls, even when we do. Faith always picks us back up (assurance), takes and sees us through whatever comes our way (confidence), and leads us to go farther than we ever thought we could because we understand we can do all things though Christ, who strengthens us.

> Lord, may our courage in You always prevail, as our confidence in You avails, and lead us to a greater understanding of our possibilities when we are in You and You in us. Help us to truly walk by faith today! Amen.

Day 4

Faith Will Always Defend Us

When they came to the crowd, a man came up to Jesus, falling on his knees before Him and saying, Lord, have mercy on my son, for he is a lunatic and is very ill; for he often falls into the fire and often into the water. I brought him to Your disciples, and they could not cure him." And Jesus answered and said, "You unbelieving and perverted generation, how long shall I be with you? How long shall I put up with you? Bring him here to Me." And Jesus rebuked him, and the demon came out of him, and the boy was cured at once. Then the disciples came to Jesus privately and said, "Why could we not drive it out?" And He *said to them, "Because of the littleness of your faith; for truly I say to you, if you have faith the size of a mustard seed, you will say to this mountain, 'Move from here to there,' and it will move; and nothing will be impossible to you."

—Matthew 17:14–20

As we learn to walk by faith, we must know what faith can and will do. There are some things that we can always count on with every step of faith we take, and today we will talk about three of the seven things that faith in God will always do.

In our text, we find a worried dad who is greatly concerned about his son's behavior. The son's behavior had been erratic, to say the least. This dad is so desperate for help that he is worried sick. The boy was acting much like someone who has epilepsy, but during that time, no one knew about any such illness. The dad did not know the cause of the behavior, so he was feeling very uneasy as the people of that day believed that some evil power had suddenly taken hold of his son. So that daddy went looking for help, and he first approached the disciples, who he found to be no help at all. Therefore, he then goes to find Jesus.

Jesus expresses His disappointment and frustration at the people's lack of faith, including his disciples. Jesus then drives out the demon plaguing the boy, and he was made whole again. The disciples wondered, if it was that easy, why couldn't they heal the boy? After all, Jesus had allowed them to do their share of healing on their missionary excursions. So Jesus told them, "It is because you have so little faith." Jesus goes on to tell them that even the smallest amount of faith in Him could make them move mountains.

Jesus's words were tough to swallow for the disciples because they had grown accustomed to going through all the motions, so they did not even realize that their faith had dwindled. Jesus was saying, "Nothing would be impossible for you if you would have simply trusted me." How is your portrait of faith looking? Are you truly walking by faith, or would Jesus find you simply going through the motions?

Jesus's words, of course, are not a "complete freedom" to ask for anything that comes to mind. It is not an invitation to manipulate God or His word to get what we want; on the contrary, Jesus's words are a call for us to completely trust Him. He is calling us to know that no matter what happens, He has our best interests at heart. This type of faith is always accompanied by a deep love for God. It has his best interest at heart every time. It is what brings joy and peace into our lives.

If God's power isn't working in you and through you, then it is possible that just like the disciples, you have a lack of faith. Remember, faith is unquestioning belief, complete trust or confidence, and loyalty. Faith is the confident assurance that what God tells is true has and will happen. Faith is not a feeling or emotion. Faith is the foundation of our relationship with God. It is surety that does not rest on logical proof or material evidence, but faith is understanding that God did everything described in His word and will do everything He promised. Faith is not something we have, as much as the way we live.

Faith will always lead to salvation. "For by grace you were saved through faith" (Eph. 2:8). We're not saved by faith, but by grace. However, faith is the funnel through which the grace of God flows.

Faith will always defend us. "Taking up the shield of faith, wherewith you will be able to quench all the fiery darts of the wicked one" (Eph. 6:16). The Roman armor included pieces such as a helmet and a breastplate, but the major piece of defensive equipment that a Roman soldier used was his trusty shield. Many a club, arrow, and sword would be deflected by the shield. The shield never did the soldier any good if the soldier never picked it up. The survival of a soldier is bleak without a shield. Christians are constantly under attack. The devil walks about like a roaring lion seeking whomever he may devour. Not to mention the attacks of the flesh that we are attacked with daily. Our faith is meant to be a constant defender. But if we never pick it up, it will be of no use.

Faith will always provide. "And they that know My Name will put their trust in Me; for I have not forsaken those who seek me" (Ps. 9:10). Faith is no if-then proposition. Like, Lord, if you give me a new car, I will drive to church twice a week, or if we are growing in the Lord and placing our trust and faith in Him, then He will never leave us nor forsake us. No, Jesus says in Matthew 6 that we should consider the lilies of the field and how they grow; they never strive, and neither do they run around like a chicken with its head cut off. Even Solomon in all his glory was not displayed like one of these. So if God is the one who puts clothes on the grass of the field, which is here today and gone tomorrow, why would he not provide much more for you?

Lord, I thank you that when our faith is solely in You, that it is a faith that we can always count on. And, Lord, please help us to never be lacking in faith, but may our faith in You lead us to walk in Your power always. Amen.

Day 5

Walking by Faith Isn't Easy

Enter by the narrow gate. For the gate is wide and
the way is easy that leads to destruction, and those
who enter by it are many. For the gate is narrow
and the way is hard that leads to life, and those
who find it are few.

—Matthew 7:13–14 (ESV)

Walking by faith is difficult mainly because of two things:
First, we don't know where to begin. Faith begins by
choosing the correct gate and "looking to Jesus, the founder
and perfector of our faith, who for the joy that was set
before him endured the cross, despising the shame, and
is seated at the right hand of the throne of God" (Heb.
12:2, ESV). There are two gates. One leads to righteousness.
This gate is narrow. Jesus told us that this is the only gate
that leads to life. This obviously means that it is the gate
that leads men to heaven. "For the gate is narrow and the
way is hard that leads to life, and those who find it are
few." This gate is narrow, and it is hard to enter through
it. This is a surprise to most of us who have been taught
that the way to heaven is easy. We have been taught that
all we have to do to be saved is say we believe in Jesus.
There is a great difference between what men are teaching
today and what Jesus taught. Jesus tells us that not many

people will choose the narrow gate. Sure, as we find out in Matthew 7:21, a lot of people will say that they entered through it because they said they believed, but there will be no repentance and there will be no evidence of a changed life or heart. Jesus said, "Even the demons believe." Going in through this straight and narrow gate will be tough because far too many people don't want a changed life; they just want the fire insurance. When they actually count the cost of following Jesus, they choose the other gate. It is much easier, and it is a place where everything is acceptable. It is easy to find and the gate is wide, but the narrow gate, Jesus says, "Few will find it." It takes the total sacrifice of handing our lives over to Jesus. This too is a surprise to many. We believe that most people in this world are saved because they say that they believe in God or even Jesus. I believe that is why Jesus tells us in Matthew 7:16 that we will know the ones who are saved "by their fruit." There are many people who think wrongly that they can continue in any lifestyle that they want and be saved. Or believe in the God they have fashioned in their mind to suit their way of life. They wrongly think that without repentance and obediently following Jesus that God will forgive their every step of disobedience. It is true that once a person is saved, they cannot be plucked from the Father's hand, but Jesus is the only way.

Repentance and faith can be understood as "two sides of the same coin." It is impossible to place our faith in Jesus

Christ as the Savior without first changing our mind about who we are, who He is, and what He has done. We are sinners. The wages of our sin is a death penalty that we earned on our own and we deserve, but Jesus died for us while we were up to our necks in sin. He rose again so that we can have eternal life. He paid the complete price for our redemption, and Jesus is the gate that we must enter to receive forgiveness of our sins and eternal life. Whether our repentance is from willful rejection or repentance from ignorance or disinterest, the commonality is found in a complete change of mind. Biblical repentance, in relation to salvation, is changing our mind from rejection of Christ (refusing to obey) to faith in Christ (surrendering to a life of wholehearted obedience).

Second, we don't know where to go. That is what Thomas so honestly expressed to Jesus in John 14. Jesus responded to him and the other disciples by saying, "Let not your hearts be troubled. Believe in God; believe also in me" (John 14:1, ESV).

> "In my Father's house are many rooms. If it were not so, would I have told you that I go to prepare a place for you? And if I go and prepare a place for you, I will come again and will take you to myself, that where I am you may be also. And you know the way to where I am going." Thomas said to him, "Lord, we do not know where you are going. How can we know the way?" Jesus said to him, "I am the

way, and the truth, and the life. No one comes to the Father except through me. If you had known me, you would have known my Father also. From now on you do know him and have seen him." (John 14:2–7, ESV)

Jesus is the Gate to Heaven or the narrow way. Not a single person can enter the narrow gate to righteousness without coming through Jesus Christ. Jesus is the only Way. Jesus is the path that we are to choose every single day. He is the Way to where we should go, He is the only Truth, and we waste our time and our lives looking any other place. Jesus is life, and without him, the only thing that is certain is death. We are to move toward Jesus every single moment of the day.

Everyone who believes that Jesus is the Christ has been born of God, and everyone who loves the Father loves whoever has been born of him. By this we know that we love the children of God, when we love God and obey his commandments. For this is the love of God, that we keep his commandments. And his commandments are not burdensome. For everyone who has been born of God overcomes the world. And this is the victory that has overcome the world—*our faith*. Who is it that overcomes the world except the one who believes that Jesus is the Son of God? (1 John 5:1–5, italics mine).

The one who believes will "deny themselves daily and take up their cross and follow Jesus wherever He leads" (Luke 9:23). Which gate will you choose?

> Lord, help us to wholeheartedly trust you. Lord, we know for sure that no one can take us from Your hand, and by our fruit we can know that we are truly Yours. Lord, we know that being saved is not having it all together, but changing our mind and wholeheartedly surrendering to You. Thank You for paying the price for all of our sins, Lord Jesus, and may we surrender to the change of mind, change of life, and change of destiny that You are preparing for us. Amen.

2

Faith Is One Directional

Walking by faith is not an easy journey. On the journey of faith, we are often faced with many challenges, trials, troubles, temptations, and inconveniences. I would like to share with you a story from a friend named Derrick who shares his and his family's journey of faith thus far. Meagan will share her personal journey in another chapter.

Derrick's Story

I'm really not sure how or even where to start. My journey of faith has had many twist and turns. It took selflessness, sacrifice, and leaving the past behind to move in the right direction. That direction is toward God. God has done a complete 180 with my life.

Satan really took hold of me around the age of twenty. All through high school, I was a considered a good kid as I hardly got into any trouble at all. Taking the occasional drink in high school was basically the extent of my troubles. When was nineteen, I met Meagan, who would eventually be my wife. She is one of the best things that has ever happened to me, but a couple months after we met, we began to drink heavily and use pot. This new lifestyle would consume us both for about four years. It seemed as though all we did was work to pay bills and for our addictions. Then Brylie was born. When this new baby entered the picture, we dropped the habit for a long while, but then we began to drink just a little. It did not take long until our addictions consumed us once again. Every weekend we would spend thirty or forty dollars on alcohol. Then my second child was born, my son, Brody. After he was born, we hardly had enough money for drinking, so we went back to smoking. Not as much though, but any at all is more than we should have.

As I look back, I remember August 2013. At this time, Meagan and I had only been married about three months, and we were both miserable. Sure, we loved each other, but we could hardly stand to be around one another. In fact, we couldn't even stand being in the same room together. She and I would go days without even speaking to one another unless it was about our kids. Things were really tough. They had escalated to the point that we would send messages to one another daily about getting a divorce. When I felt that life could not get any worse, the worst thing happened: Meagan tried to kill herself. I praise God that she failed, but this terrified me. On the outside, I kept a good appearance and tried to keep a level head, but on the inside, I was hurt, angry, and frustrated. I kept asking myself, *How could she do that to me, our babies, or to herself?* I then began to blame myself. If only I had been the husband that she needed me to be.

From that day forward, I became dedicated to being the husband that Meagan needed me to be, and that is something that I have worked on daily. Nevertheless, there was still something missing.

As I was growing up, my mom and dad did not display an outward religious appearance, even though it was understood that they believed in God. We didn't go to church much, if at all that I can remember. Faith wasn't something that we really discussed or talked about; it was assumed. I always figured I knew there is a God, so I am okay.

As for Meagan, her mom and dad were very faithful Christians. They were accustomed to attending church, and her dad has served many years as a deacon in a local Baptist church. Nevertheless, we were at what seemed to be life's lowest point.

Out of desperation, the following March 24, the kids and I went to church. We sang a song called "Whom Shall I Fear" that talked about the God of angel armies. I could not stop thinking about the words to that song, and that's the day I committed to start attending church regularly and getting my family into church. One month later, we moved back to Diana, and on May 14, I surrendered my life to the Lord. Eleven days later on May 25, our one-year wedding anniversary, I was baptized.

I have learned so much since becoming a Christian, and I am so thankful that God was so patient with me and my family. It is all because of Him that we made it through. It is all because of Him that I now walk by faith. I have done nothing to deserve the love, grace, and mercy that He has shown me, but through Him and through a commitment to His Word, God has changed my life and my family. As I surrender, God is growing me into the person He wants me to be, the husband my wife needs me to be, and the daddy my kids need me to be. God has taken my marriage to new heights and new places we never thought possible.

The scripture that we rely on when we talk about our marriage is Ruth 1:16–17.

> But Ruth said, "Do not urge me to leave you or to return from following you. For where you go I will go, and where you lodge I will lodge. Your people shall be my people, and your God my God. Where you die I will die, and there will I be buried. May the Lord do so to me and more also if anything but death parts me from you."

I have learned that the best two things a person can do is to love God with all their heart, all their soul, all their mind, and all their strength; and love others as themselves (Luke 10:27). God's greatest gift was Jesus, and there is *no* denying that, but when He took that rib from Adam, I know without a shadow of a doubt that he had Meagan in mind for me. I know that I need to love her like Jesus loves me. Today, I walk by faith because Jesus saved me, gives me strength, and loves me, but it takes denying myself and taking up my cross daily and following Him (Luke 9:23).

Derrick realized that God only leads in one direction, and that direction is toward Him every single time. There is never an instance where we must go any other direction. Our lives are also to be built on a sure foundation, which is the foundation of His Word, and Jesus is the Word. When God reaches down and saves us, this is a life-changing event that takes hold of us for an eternity, just as He did with Derrick. Derrick is determined to walk by faith for the rest of his life. He knows that Jesus is the only way, the only truth, and the only life from firsthand experience. Walking by faith was meant to be a one-directional walk, and that is exactly what God has made Derrick's walk as he has committed his life to obeying and following Jesus no matter the cost and wherever He leads.

Day 6

Walking by Faith Leads to One Destination

> Beware of false prophets, who come to you in
> sheep's clothing but inwardly are ravenous wolves.
> You will recognize them by their fruits. Are grapes
> gathered from thorn bushes, or figs from thistles?
> So, every healthy tree bears good fruit, but the
> diseased tree bears bad fruit. A healthy tree cannot
> bear bad fruit, nor can a diseased tree bear good
> fruit. Every tree that does not bear good fruit is
> cut down and thrown into the fire. Thus you will
> recognize them by their fruits.
>
> —Matthew 7:15–20 (ESV)

In life, we can say what we want to follow Christ, but there are only two ways and two destinations. Jesus is the way to heaven and eternity. This gate has one entrance or gate, and its one destination is heaven. The other gate is choosing this world and the father of this world. This gate is wide, and many will find it. This gate leads to destruction, and there are many entrances. To walk by faith, we must find the narrow gate and stay on that road. However, scripture tells us that there will be people who will try to pull us off that path when we don't recognize the difference in the fruit because we do no know what God's word says.

In verse 15, we find that there are also only two types of people and two types of fruit. There are two types of people: those who are saved and those who are not. We call those who are saved Christian and those who are not non-Christian. But we have watered down the term *Christian* today to fit anyone who believes in God. Sometimes we even add in and know who Jesus is, but the word *Christian* was only meant to describe the followers of Jesus Christ. Jesus is the only Way (to heaven and the Father), the only Truth (the Word, the measure of accountability), and the only Life (abundant life, fruit-bearing life, and eternal life). To be a Christian, to live the Christian life, and to truly be saved is a life found only in Jesus. It is a life of walking by faith and producing fruit. There are no "kinda" saved or almost saved people out there. We either went through the gate of righteousness (Jesus), or we take the second gate that leads to destruction. If we took the gate to heaven (Jesus), then our lives will be completely changed. The Christian life is a life of honoring God, following Jesus, abiding in the vine, and allowing the Holy Spirit to produce fruit in and through us.

Our text today says, "Beware of false prophets, who come to you in sheep's clothing but inwardly are ravenous wolves. You will recognize them by their fruits. Are grapes gathered from thornbushes, or figs from thistles? So, every healthy tree bears good fruit, but the diseased tree bears bad fruit. A healthy tree cannot bear bad fruit, nor can a diseased tree bear good fruit. Every tree that does not bear good fruit is cut down and thrown into the fire. Thus you will recognize them by their fruits" (Matt. 7:15–20, ESV).

We are to be able to recognize false prophets (Matt. 7:15), false Christs (Matt. 24:24), false apostles (2 Cor. 11:13), false brethren (Gal. 2:4, 2 Cor. 11:20), false teachers (2 Pet. 2:1), and deceitful workers (2 Cor. 11:13). In other words, we will recognize the saved from the unsaved by the fruit being produced in their lives. Jesus told us, "You will know these people by their fruit!" Good fruit can only come "by Jesus Christ." Fruit that comes from any other tree, even though it may speak about God or even talk of Jesus, can and will only produce false or bad fruit.

The bad fruit will be produced through those in sheep's clothing. In other words, they will look like sheep. They may even be good people. They will talk about Jesus and even claim to do things in His Name. However, they will be selfish; they will restructure God's word to soothe their ego or to accomplish their own agendas. They will give off the appearance of the sheep, but they will destroy instead of edify. They will treat the church as a business. They will kill people with the Word instead of using it as God intended to bring restoration and life. They will demand their own comfort at the expense of the Kingdom of God. Most of all, the things they do will not be done in agape love, but instead to uphold tradition or out of selfish motives. We will know these people by their fruit, and if we can't recognize them, then they will entice us and lure us to the pit.

Those who choose Jesus as the only way always remember to pursue Him with all their heart and to abide only in

Him. One who is saved will passionately pursue growth in their relationship with Jesus and then get busy doing what He has prepared for them. The fruit of the Spirit is called the fruit of the spirit because fruit is only born through the Holy Spirit. The Holy Spirit is the one raising us to new life. The new Spirit, the new nature, is Christ in us. We are to abide in Christ, and the Holy Spirit produces good fruit through those who are saved. Christ in us is the way that good fruit can and will be produced through us. We will know that He is alive and well in us and in others by the fruit being produced.

> Lord, help us to realize that those who have been redeemed are those who have gone through the gate to heaven, Jesus. Lord, help us to stop watering down the Christian lifestyle by using it as a term for anyone who says that they know God. Lord, may your good fruit be vibrant and alive in the life of the redeemed as they wholeheartedly abide in You alone because the fruit is how others will know that we are Yours. Amen.

Day 7

Walking by Faith Is the Way for Life

But the fruit of the Spirit is love, joy, peace,
longsuffering, kindness, goodness, faithfulness,
gentleness, self-control. Against such there is no
law. And those who are Christ's have crucified the
flesh with its passions and desires. If we live in the
Spirit, let us also walk in the Spirit.

—Galatians 5:22–25

Over the past few days, we have talked about the truths Jesus left us about walking by faith. We found that in this life, there are only two gates to choose from, and there are only two destinations each gate leads to. We further found that Jesus makes it clear that there are only two kinds of people with each kind producing one particular kind of fruit.

When we walk by faith, we live as though Jesus is the only way, the only truth, and the only life because He is, and we are only truly walking by faith by choosing Jesus. Walking by faith is choosing, following, keeping our eyes on, and trusting Jesus every time. Truly walking by faith is by no means taking the easy way in life, but it is the only way that leads to a life filled with hope, love, peace, joy, grace, mercy, and the list goes on. Taking the gate to heaven means that there will be change, a new life, and a new way of living. Taking the narrow gate is walking in the truth and finding life. Taking the narrow gate will take humility, surrender, obedience, and sacrifice. That is what Jesus meant when He stated, "If you are going to be my follower (going down the same path with Me)"; then it will take "denying yourself and taking up your cross" to do so. Only those who choose the first gate are the redeemed, the saved, and you will know them because when you look at them, you see Jesus in them and living through them, producing good fruit.

It is impossible for the one wholeheartedly walking by faith to have one foot in one gate and the other foot in another gate. We can't choose the combo meal. We either choose the first gate, we are saved, our destination is heaven, and we bear good fruit. Sure this pathway is hard, and not many will choose this gate. Those who choose this path may slip, fall, and stumble, but Jesus is right there to pick them back up. Most people will choose the second gate because this gate "is wide and the way is easy," but it leads to destruction. "Those who enter by it are many." The only path to heaven is through Jesus, but the gate to destruction is so wide that it makes it hard to find the narrow gate—Jesus. Anything can go through the broad gate, and this is the gate that the second type of people go through. These people are the unsaved. Their only destination is hell, and their fruit is bad, fake, or false. Sure, many of these people on this path attempt to look like the people on the narrow path, but "by their fruit we know" that they are not saved.

Putting it simply, the fruit is a changed life or an unchanged life. Therefore, a Christ-centered life is a life where we have died to ourselves so that Christ can live through us (Gal. 2:19–20). It costs giving everything over to Jesus. The life in Christ is a life that seeks to satisfy God rather than self. It is a life walking by faith because our central theme, focus, and priority is Jesus alone.

What does the fruit produced by real Christian look like? Galatians 5:22–25 says,

> But the fruit of the Spirit is love, joy, peace, long-suffering, kindness, goodness, faithfulness, gentleness, self-control. Against such there is no law. And those who are Christ's have crucified the flesh with its passions and desires. If we live in the Spirit, let us also walk in the Spirit.

Because Jesus Christ lives in us, we are to allow Him to live through us. When we do so, we are living according to the new man. By the way, those who are truly saved no longer live by the old man but the new. When we are living according to the new man, we produce the fruit given or produced by the Holy Spirit. We have a new life, and we walk that way. We have a totally new character, which is the character of the new man. Ephesians 2:10 says, "For we are His workmanship, created in Christ Jesus for good works, which God prepared beforehand that we should walk in them."

God has already prepared the good works in which we should walk. That is what it means to walk by faith. I praise God that He has already gifted each one of us uniquely, and like a tree planted by the water, we are destined to bear fruit. All that we have to do is to walk in what God has already prepared. We don't and can't manufacture it on our own as those who entered the wrong gate try to do.

So how do we bear godly fruit in a world that hates Christians? How do we walk by faith? Philippians 1:9–11 says,

> And this I pray, that your love may abound still more and more in knowledge and all discernment, that you may approve the things that are excellent, that you may be sincere and without offense till the day of Christ, being filled with the fruits of righteousness which are by Jesus Christ, to the glory and praise of God.

The fruits of righteousness "are by Jesus Christ," not a result of our own power or ability. Jesus explains this in John 15:4–8. Jesus says that

> He is the vine and we are the branches. He says we are to abide in Him, and He in us. As the branch cannot bear fruit of itself, unless it abides in the vine, neither can you, unless you abide in Me. Jesus continues as He says, I am the vine, you are the

branches. He who abides in Me, and I in him, bears much fruit; for without Me you can do nothing! By this My Father is glorified, that you bear much fruit; so you will be My disciples.

Bearing much good fruit is a requirement for those who belong to Jesus. That is why Jesus said, "By their fruit you will know them." We only bear fruit as we grow ever closer to Jesus and completely abide in the Vine. Remember, we are not the Vine. Jesus is! We are simply the branches. It is impossible for a branch to bring forth fruit, unless it abides in the vine. As we walk by faith, we are simply vessels through which He will produce fruit. Therefore we are to be ministering and pursuing the good works that God has prepared for us. This requires a passionate relationship with Jesus. The aim of our life is to please Him. Therefore, we do not focus on the fruit or our own works, but our aim and focus is Jesus Christ.

Lord, help us to pursue You with all our heart and grow in our relationship with You. Lord, help us to get busy doing what You have prepared for us and bear much good fruit. Amen.

Day 8

Faith Is Built on the Right Foundation

Everyone then who hears these words of mine and
does them will be like a wise man who built his
house on the rock. And the rain fell, and the floods
came, and the winds blew and beat on that house,
but it did not fall, because it had been founded on
the rock. And everyone who hears these words of
mine and does not do them will be like a foolish
man who built his house on the sand. And the rain
fell, and the floods came, and the winds blew and
beat against that house, and it fell, and great was
the fall of it.

—Matthew 7:24–27 (ESV)

When we are walking by faith, then we will completely live
life in Christ, and He will live through us. When we are
walking by faith, then we will know that there are only *two
ways or two gates* (verses 13–14), *two types of people* (verse
15), *two destinations* (verses 13–14, 21), *two kinds of trees and
two kinds of fruit* (verses 17–19, Luke 6:43–44), *and today
we will talk about the truth that there are only two foundations
and two types of builders* (Matthew 7:24–27, ESV).

In this life, the foundation our life is built upon makes
all the difference in the world. In fact, Proverbs 24:3 says,
"By wisdom a house is built, and by understanding it is
established." This passage of scripture refers to our life

as our house. Therefore, it references our life in a more personal manner.

In Matthew 7:24–27, Jesus tells a parable that contrasts two builders: one wise and one foolish. He compares two foundations, one strong and able to withstand any storm, and one shifty, shaky, and unable to withstand even a moderate storm.

Jesus's use of building metaphors should not surprise us because He was a carpenter by trade. Therefore, Jesus knew the difference between a well-built house and a poorly built house. This story is for you and me. Building a house is a simple analogy for building a life. In our walk, our life, or our faith is the builder. We are either a wise builder or a foolish builder. We will either build on the strong foundation of the Word of God, or we will build on the weak and frail foundation of public opinion, tradition, or the world (which are all the same foundation, weak and frail). Yes, in life we each choose the foundation that our life will be built upon, and again, Jesus only gives us two options.

Being a wise builder and building our life on the strong foundation (Matt. 7:24–25), Jesus says, "is only possible by obeying His every word." Jesus says, "Everyone who hears these words of Mine and acts on them, may be compared to a wise man who built his house on the rock." Jesus reveals to us that His words are intended for all people for all times. Yes, even today. We begin by hearing His words. In other words, we must expose our self to the truth of God's word. This is accomplished by reading the Bible, by reading Christian books, by attending worship, by getting involved in small groups and Bible studies with Christian friends, or by taking Christian educational classes. Jesus says that every area of our life is to be built upon the foundation of faithful obedience to His word. Jesus urges us to hear His words, and then He says that we are to obey or must act upon His words.

Did you know that when we hear the word of God that we do one of two things? We act upon or obey His word and it becomes a firm foundation, or we disobey His word and build upon the sand. If we are going to build on a strong, firm, solid, and dependable foundation, then we must do what Jesus tells us through His word to do. Hearing His words is not sufficient enough for building the foundation that will prevail through any storm.

Matthew 7:25 tells us why it's so critical to build on the strong foundation of obeying Jesus's every word. Jesus says, "And the rain fell, and the floods came, and the winds blew and slammed against that house; and yet it did not fall, for it had been founded on the rock." Notice that Jesus does not say "if the rain falls" or "if the floods come" or "if the winds blow," but instead He says that they will come. Therefore, building on the right foundation is critical to life. Make no mistake, obedience to God's word does not mean that we will not find ourselves in the middle of any storm, but instead it means that we will be able to withstand every storm because our life is built upon the right foundation.

On the other side of the coin, we can destroy our life by building it on the wrong foundation (Matt. 7:26–27). In Matthew 7:26, Jesus says, "Everyone who hears these words of Mine and does not act on them, will be like a foolish man who built his house on the sand." Therefore, the opposite of a wise man is a foolish man. The Greek word for *foolish* is *moros*. In other words, a person who disregards Jesus's words is called foolish, stupid, and a moron. Why? Because that person didn't build on the rock of Jesus's words.

We must be the wise builder who builds their life upon Jesus's every word. It is even more critical today, especially in a world that seems to be drifting farther and farther away from a life built upon a strong foundation. As a result, we see destroyed lives, marriages, and relationships. Make no mistake, the storms are growing stronger with cancer, heart disease, and many other diseases seeking to devour life. These are big storms, but building on the right foundation is critical for even the small storms lest our foundation be washed away over time.

First Peter 2:9 says, "But you are a chosen generation, a royal priesthood, a holy nation, His own special people, that you may proclaim the praises of Him who called you out of darkness into His marvelous light," and 1 Peter 2:5 says, "You also, as living stones, are being built up a spiritual house, a holy priesthood, to offer up spiritual sacrifices acceptable to God through Jesus Christ."

Lord, help us to be wise builders who build our lives in wholehearted obedience to Your word alone. Amen.

Day 9

Faith Walks Only in the Truth

I tell you, he will give justice to them speedily.
Nevertheless, when the Son of Man comes, will he
find faith on earth?

—Luke 18:8 (ESV)

The hardest thing about walking by faith for most people is believing the truth. We were born into a dark, dying, and lost world, but God has had plans from the beginning to rescue us from this world. So He sent His Son, Jesus who died and rose again for whosoever would choose to place their complete faith in Him. Faith is being in the world, but not of the world. Faith leads us to live for Jesus in the middle of calm, chaos, and condemnation.

We have discussed so far that faith is believing in what is true. Faith has four elements: being convinced of the truth, being certain of reality, having evidence of unseen things, and believing, hoping in, embracing, and seizing the truth at all costs. Hebrews 11:1 says, "Now faith is the substance of things hoped for, the evidence of things not seen." In other words, faith in Christ makes us certain of realities we can't even see. Faith is well-grounded assurance in our only hope, Jesus alone. Faith is the conviction of the reality that everything about the Father, Son, and Holy Spirit that we do not see is true. But even though faith requires being convinced that what we believe in is true, simply knowing the truth is only half of faith. Faith is hoping for, embracing, seizing, and obeying God's word.

In Luke 17:5, the apostles said to Jesus, "Increase our faith!" And Jesus replied, "If you have faith as small as a mustard seed, you can say to this mulberry tree, 'Be uprooted and planted in the sea,' and it will obey you."

We must realize that simply believing is not an accurate synonym for faith. Our belief becomes faith when it leads us to the light. Sure, there are times when belief alone is what is required. These are times when there is no time for evidence collection, time to wait, to hear, or time for complete certainty. During those times, we are to simply believe. For example, when Peter was commanded to walk on the water, Jesus was telling him, "Peter, don't think, just act, and keep your eyes on Me!" Believing is enough, and it is what God requires in moments of human weakness, but don't mistake believing for faith. It is faith that makes us strong. Faith is the state of being completely convinced by our only hope, Jesus.

Contrary to popular teaching, faith is not mental delusion, presumption, or self-deception, but it is completely the work of the Holy Spirit and the Word of God. Romans 10:17 says, "Faith comes by hearing the message, and the message is heard through the word of Christ."

C. S. Lewis said, "We must not encourage in ourselves or others any tendency to work up a subjective state which, if we succeeded, we should describe as 'faith,' with the idea that this will somehow insure the granting of our prayer. The state of mind which desperate desire working on a strong imagination can manufacture is not faith in the Christian sense. It is a feat of psychological gymnastics."

Belief separated from the truth is not faith at all. Believing in what is not from God is not faith at all and is in fact a lie. Believing in our mind, thoughts, or the philosophies of others is nothing more than deception if not conformed to the Word of God. Just because we call something faith does not make it so.

A. W. Tozer said,

> I do not recall another period when "faith" was as popular as it is today. If only we believe hard enough we'll make it somehow. So goes the popular chant. What you believe is not important. Only believe… What is overlooked in all this is that faith is good only when it engages truth; when it is made to rest upon falsehood it can and often does lead to eternal tragedy. For it is not enough that we believe; we must believe the right thing about the right One.

Second Thessalonians 2:10–11, says, "They perish because they refuse to love the truth and so be saved. For this reason God sends them a powerful delusion so that they will believe the lie." Too many of us no longer walk by faith because we have believed the lie. We have failed to understand that it is sin to doubt God, and it is also sin to believe things that don't lead us to honor and glorify God. Faith never means being gullible. True faith, found in a healthy heart for God, will always keep dead and poisonous matter out.

The preeminence of Christ is what we believe and what leads us to faith.

> He is the image of the invisible God, the firstborn of all creation. For by him all things were created, in heaven and on earth, visible and invisible, whether thrones or dominions or rulers or authorities—all things were created through him and for him. And he is before all things, and in him all things hold together. And he is the head of the body, the church. He is the beginning, the firstborn from the dead, that in everything he might be preeminent. For in him all the fullness of God was pleased to dwell, and through him to reconcile to himself all things, whether on earth or in heaven, making peace by the blood of his cross. And you, who once were alienated and hostile in mind, doing evil deeds, he has now reconciled in his body of flesh by his death, in order to present you holy and blameless and above reproach before him, if indeed you continue in the faith, stable and steadfast, not shifting from the hope of the gospel that you heard, which has been proclaimed in all creation under heaven. (Col. 1:15–23, esv)

Hebrews 11:6 (NIV) says, "Without faith it is impossible to please God." The question is when Jesus comes back for us, will He find faith in you?

Lord, help us to walk by faith. Amen.

Day 10

Faith Realizes God's Provision

His divine power has granted to us all things that pertain to life and godliness, through the knowledge of him who called us to his own glory and excellence, by which he has granted to us his precious and very great promises, so that through them you may become partakers of the divine nature, having escaped from the corruption that is in the world because of sinful desire. For this very reason, make every effort to supplement your faith with virtue, and virtue with knowledge, and knowledge with self-control, and self-control with steadfastness, and steadfastness with godliness, and godliness with brotherly affection, and brotherly affection with love. For if these qualities are yours and are increasing, they keep you from being ineffective or unfruitful in the knowledge of our Lord Jesus Christ. For whoever lacks these qualities is so nearsighted that he is blind, having forgotten that he was cleansed from his former sins. Therefore, brothers, be all the more diligent to confirm your calling and election, for if you practice these qualities you will never fall. For in this way there will be richly provided for you an entrance into the eternal kingdom of our Lord and Savior Jesus Christ. Therefore I intend always to remind you of these qualities, though you know them and are established in the truth that you have.

> I think it right, as long as I am in this body, to stir you up by way of reminder, since I know that the putting off of my body will be soon, as our Lord Jesus Christ made clear to me. And I will make every effort so that after my departure you may be able at any time to recall these things. (2 Pet. 1:3–15, ESV)

We have talked about faith in great length. We have discussed what faith is and what faith is not, and we have talked about building a life of faith, but God is leading me to lead you to take a step back. We are going to step back and capture two truths. The first truth is that God provided everything necessary to live the godly life, and the second truth is we must adequately count the cost of following Jesus and, thereby, walking by faith.

Our focal text will be 2 Peter 1:3–15.

> His divine power has granted to us all things that pertain to life and godliness, through the knowledge of him who called us to his own glory and excellence, by which he has granted to us his precious and very great promises, so that through them you may become partakers of the divine nature, having escaped from the corruption that is in the world because of sinful desire (2 Pet. 1:3–4).

God has provided everything we need to live the life of faith that He calls us to live. The only real obstacles to walking by faith are sin and self. Nevertheless, God has provided everything we need to rid our lives of those two obstacles. It has always been God's plan to be our everything.

What happened? How did we get to the point of self-reliance, self-centeredness, self-ambition, and sinfully desiring fame and fortune over walking by faith? Why are our local churches and lives walking from one business transaction to the other instead of walking by faith? Have you noticed that for most local churches and the individual believers that make up those churches, their lives can be described by three words: "business as usual." I believe that the answer to all these questions is we have had the breath knocked out of us!

We must remember that our body and soul were created by Jesus's hands in Genesis 2:7, and then He breathed life or the Spirit into man. "Then the LORD God formed the man of dust from the ground and breathed into his nostrils the breath of life, and the man became a living creature" (Gen. 2:7, ESV). What we must notice is that there was no life until Jesus breathed the Holy Spirit into our life and gave us life. The same is true for the church, the saved, the redeemed, or the Body of Christ. Jesus is the Creator and giver of life, but the Holy Spirit is the provider and power for life, and we have had that breath of life knocked right out of us by sin because of the flesh and the enticements of the devil.

In the beginning, God was provider and protector, and He was absolutely everything because the Holy Spirit had complete control of Adam and Eve because they walked with God and stayed close to God and because God breathed life into them. They did not need or want for anything, but in Genesis 3, they were enticed by Satan, and their flesh gave in to temptation, and as a result, the life, the breath, and the Spirit of God was knocked right out of them. Since that is true, then Adam and Eve were moving around and functioning, but they were spiritually dead. While in our sin and without Jesus Christ breathing life into us, we are spiritually dead. There is no life without the power and the presence of the Holy Spirit, and there is no Holy Spirit in our life without it being breathed into our life by Jesus.

In our sin we are dead. The body and the soul are lifeless without Jesus breathing life into them. That is what we are without Christ. Too many local churches have shut Jesus out with their narcissistic hearts, and when we shut Jesus out, then we are lifeless and dead. Jesus brought the very breath back to us that had been knocked out of us by our sin. We have all sinned and therefore are dead without Christ (Rom. 3:23, 6:23). Sin continues to knock the breath of us unless we turn from our sin and stop feeding the flesh and turn to Jesus. The Spirit gives life to the soul, and the soul gives life to the body.

What must we do to get back to the life of faith? We pray, repent, confess, and believe. Second Chronicles 7:14 says, "If my people who are called by my name humble themselves, and pray and seek my face and turn from their wicked ways, then I will hear from heaven and will forgive their sin and heal their land."

> Lord, we praise You today that Your divine power has granted to us all things that pertain to life and godliness, through the knowledge of You who called us to Your own glory and excellence, by which You have granted to us Your precious and very great promises, so that through them we may become partakers of the divine nature, having escaped from the corruption that is in the world because of sinful desire. Lord, breathe life back into us, and, Holy Spirit, may we surrender to Your revelation of Jesus in our life, and may You bring life and guidance to us for Your glory alone. Amen.

Faith is Extraordinarily Reassuring

Walking by faith is always extraordinarily reassuring. God loves to show us His signs and wonders. The problem is that we are infrequently walking close enough to Him to see them. Walking by faith often takes us through the valley so that we can see God and allow Him to produce good fruit in and through our lives. Romans 8:28 is my favorite verse because it ensures me that we serve a limitless God who can do mighty works that we can't even fathom, but we must trust Him to work all thing our for our good and His glory.

Some friends of mine, Cori and Eddie Vest, share a supernatural story of faith where God worked all things out.

Cori, Eddie, and Robyn's Story

Cori tells their story this way: Do you believe in miracles? Would you have to see a miracle with your own eyes to believe in one? I have seen many miracles with my own eyes. I have seen God raise the dead, heal the blind, heal the deaf, heal the lame, and have unbelievers come to know Him. In Matthew 11:5, Jesus answered and said to them, "Go and report to John what you hear and see: the BLIND RECEIVE SIGHT and the lame walk, the lepers are cleansed and the deaf hear, the dead are raised up, and the POOR HAVE THE GOSPEL PREACHED TO THEM." I not only have seen how God performs miracles, but Eddie, Robyn, Ryan, and I are miracles.

At age sixteen, I experienced and lived through a very tough situation. I watched cancer destroy the best thing in my life at the time as my adorable mother lost her battle with cancer. I watched for three years as she suffered with this ugly disease. Cancer is a disease that robs and destroys many lives and families. I felt that God did not hear nor answer my prayers. I couldn't understand why God would take my mom from me and leave me without a mother. Two years later, my grandfather passed away from a sudden heart attack, and only five months after that, my grandmother followed as she also passed away from a sudden heart attack. My life seemed to be one tragedy after another, and I did not understand what God was doing.

Nevertheless, the tragedies kept coming as two years later, I received a phone call while at work to inform me that my dad was in a wreck. The voice on the phone would further state that he was life-flighted by helicopter to the hospital and that I should meet him there. All that I could do was think the worst. I knew that if he was being airlifted, his injuries had to be very bad. Little did I know, before arriving at the hospital, my dad passed away as he had a massive heart attack.

I never thought in my wildest dreams that I would experience such heartache in my lifetime. My life at that point could be summed up as one tragedy after another. I truly could not understand why God allowed all of this to happen to me. So I began to question, why me, Lord? Why am I being left alone! I now have no parents or grandparents; what am I to do? Is it because of something that I had done? Was I not living right? Was I not praying right? Was it something so wrong that I was being punished? The truth is, I couldn't ask enough whys.

As it was just me and God, I learned that God can use our suffering to draw us closer to Him. He uses all the things and events in our lives to mold us, sharpen our character, and to influence others for Him. When I was at my lowest, I remembered that God is good, just, loving, and merciful. God taught me that so often, things happen to us that we simply cannot and do not understand, but He is right there with us to see us through them. Proverbs 3:5–6 states, "Trust in the LORD with all your heart and lean not on your own understanding; in all your ways acknowledge Him, and He will make your paths straight." Genesis 50:20 reminds us that the things in life that look as though they were intended for harm, God intends them for good, and God allows them so that He can accomplish what is now being done, the saving of many lives. And if you're committed to God, He promises that He can and will take whatever pain you're experiencing and draw something good from it.

I believe that God placed Eddie in my life to help me through my sadness, aloneness, and loss. Eddie and I learned at an early stage in our marriage that as long as we have God and each other to lean on, we can conqueror the world.

Seven years passed since the last tragic event happened, and everything seemed to be going great, but on April 23, 1997, the way I saw my life going would be changed in a split second. Life as I once saw and planned it would never be the same or even close to the same. On this day, my family were victims of a fatal car accident. I had only thought I had experienced pain with the past losses, but this pain was about to be taken to an all-new level.

My husband Eddie, my daughter Robyn, my niece, and I were riding down an old country road laughing and singing to a rock-and-roll song when tragedy struck. We never saw it coming! We never even heard it coming. A sixteen-year-old driver who had only had his license for three days was driving his 4×4 dually truck drunk. Who knows why, but he turned off the headlights of his truck and attempted to jump the road we were driving on. As the dually truck went airborne, it landed on top of our truck. We rolled down an embankment. Eddie was thrown out of the truck about a hundred yards, Robyn and my niece remained in the truck, and here I was with my arm stuck under the passenger-side door as the truck lay on its side.

I was pronounced dead at the scene, but I remember hearing voices as I lay there. I heard one of the paramedics telling the other paramedic that I had no pulse, and all of a sudden, I was gone. Miraculously, five days later, to everyone's amazement, I awoke to a nurse talking softly to me. I soon learned that the nurses and doctors had already spoken to our family and friends and told them that it would be a miracle if anyone survived this traumatic accident.

I looked around the room fearfully for Eddie and Robyn, but they were not there. I had no idea what was going on as I had no memory of what happened. I didn't know why I was lying in a hospital bed. So I began asking questions. I would ask questions like what was going on and where was my family.

Little did I know, Eddie and Robyn were in the next room, but they too had suffered some substantial injuries. As Eddie and Robyn were wheeled into my room that afternoon, I learned the extent of those injuries, and I found out that my niece did not survive the wreck. Now I know today that my niece is rejoicing in heaven with our Heavenly Father, but her loss really hurt. I further learned that Eddie, Robyn, and I were on life support for approximately five days, and my husband Eddie had no memory of being married to me. He remembered our daughter Robyn, but not me. Oh, how that hurt! Eddie had been a comfort to so much of the pain that I had experienced in my past, but now he didn't even know me.

This memory loss lasted for over three months, which seemed like an eternity. The doctors believed that due to a significant lack of oxygen to the brain that Eddie would be mentally impaired. Eddie's brain had been cut and his head and face crushed. He had suffered so much head damage that his eye had popped out and his ear had been cut off. Eddie was in such bad shape, and it was not just his head. Eddie's arm had been crushed, and his leg was broken. Eddie had to undergo extensive plastic surgery to correct his facial and head trauma. The doctors placed metal plates in both the head and face. His ear was reattached, and his eye socket and face were rebuilt. He had some long-term and short-term memory loss.

Robyn had three pieces of glass stuck to the cornea of her left eye. The doctors informed us that she would be blind in the left eye. Her arm was broken, and she went through a couple of plastic surgeries for her face and chest. Robyn was unable to talk for ten days because of shock, and her brain was not communicating correctly.

I was pronounced dead at the scene. I had a broken nose, eight broken ribs, a collapsed lung, and my right arm was broken and crushed at the elbow, causing loss of movement or feeling.

Eddie and I were unable to work for over a year and had to have family members take care of us. We had numerous doctor appointments, surgeries, and physical therapy. I went through eight months of physical therapy for my arm. There was no improvement as far as movement or feeling in the arm. I would undergo nerve testing to see if the nerves would rejuvenate, and the results showed no hope of healing. The doctor would discuss our options and inform us that the best option would be to have my arm amputated because it was losing shape, and there was nothing more medically they could do.

One week prior to having the scheduled surgery on my arm, I was sitting in church. I looked down at my hand, and much to my surprise, my index finger was moving to the beat of the music. The following day I called the doctor and informed him that my finger started to move. The doctor was so surprised, but informed me that we would try physical therapy again. I began going through more treatment and enduring the agonizing pain, but I regained full strength and movement.

Robyn went through eye surgery, and the doctor told us that Robyn would be blind in her left eye due to the amount of glass stuck in the cornea of her eye. Today, Robyn sees 20/20.

I remember the nurses and doctors telling us as we were leaving the hospital that we were truly a miracle. They said that there is no medial explanation for why we had survived, especially without mental disabilities. I remember sitting with Eddie and asking him, "Why does God allow us to go through trials and tribulations? Why are we going through this? Why is God allowing this to happen to us?" These were questions that again could not be answered, but in my mind, I remember thinking about all that Job had suffered.

Job went through so much more than my family was going through, but I couldn't help but wonder, why did God test our faith this way? I can truthfully say that no matter how strong a person is in Christ, they begin to question their faith and purpose in light of tragedy.

One of the most difficult parts of the Christian life is realizing that becoming a follower and disciple of Christ does not make one immune to life's tests, trials, and tribulations. Have you ever asked yourself why a good and loving God would allow us to go through such things? I have. I have even been tempted to conclude that if He loved us, He would take all pain and sufferings away from us, not give it to us. After all, doesn't God loving us mean that our lives should be easy and comfortable?

Well, as I have learned through experience, no, it doesn't! The Bible clearly teaches that "God loves those who are His children, and He works all things together for our good" (Rom. 8:28). First Peter 1:6–7 states, "In this you greatly rejoice, even though now for a little while, if necessary, you have been distressed by various trials, that the proof of your faith, being more precious than gold which perishes, even though tested by fire, may be found to result in praise and glory and honor at the revelation of Jesus Christ."

The true believer's faith will be made sure through the trials we experience as we rest in truth that "God is us and He will never leave us nor forsake us" and that the pain won't last forever. Job 42:10 says, "The LORD restored the fortunes of Job when he prayed for his friends, and the LORD increased all that Job had twofold."

God blessed Eddie and I with a precious baby boy. You see, Eddie and I never dreamed at this time in our lives while we were still trying to heal that God would perform another miracle. God gave us our son, Ryan.

As a family, we have learned that trials develop godly character, and that enables us to "rejoice in our sufferings, because we know that suffering produces perseverance; perseverance, character; hope. And hope does not disappoint us, because God has poured out his love into our hearts by the Holy Spirit, whom he has given us" (Rom. 5:3–5).

Jesus Christ set the perfect example. "But God demonstrates His own love toward us, in that while we were yet sinners, Christ died for us" (Rom. 5:8). These verses revealed to us the very aspects of God's divine purpose. Knowing that God has a plan for me and my family led me to trust Him and completely rely on Him right in the midst of tragedy. I would never have made it without God, and neither would my family. Was it hard and did I question him? Yes, I did. But I knew God was not going to leave me or forsake me. God had a plan for us, and I just had to learn how to accept what was happening and trust Him to deliver me. Jeremiah 29:11 says, "For I know the plans I have for you, declares the LORD, plans to prosper you and not to harm you, plans to give you hope and a future."

The night of our wreck, another unexpected event was taking place at Eddie's father's home. Eddie's dad had been experiencing some heartbreaking events, and he really felt there was no hope that things would ever get better. You see, Eddie's dad had never allowed God in his heart, nor had he ever had the desire to know Jesus as His Savior. Therefore, He did not recognize what God was capable of doing. He felt lonely, helpless, and had without hope in wanting to continue his journey here on earth. Literally moments before him taking his own life, his daughter and granddaughter appeared on his doorstep, telling him of our accident. His daughter and granddaughter arrived at his home to pick him up to join the rest of the family at the hospital. When they arrived at the hospital, family and friends were gathered around, waiting for the doctors to update them on what was going on. One of our special friends was a preacher, and he had suggested that everyone gather around in prayer.

God states in Matthew 18:19, "Again I say unto you, That if two of you shall agree on earth concerning anything that they shall ask, it shall be done for them of my Father who is in heaven." Our preacher began talking to everyone, and the presence of God filled the room.

Eddie's dad began to cry. He then grabbed the preacher by the hand and proceeded to tell him of the events that took place minutes before his daughter and granddaughter appeared at his home.

It is a promise for those who love God, and the promise is that God turns everything to good, that God will somehow or other bring the best out of a bad situation for those who love him. In Romans 8:28, it states, "And we know that God causes everything to work together for the good of those who love God and are called according to his purpose for them." You see, God showed Eddie's dad the love and support that surrounds family and friends when all is gathered together for one purpose. Through this difficult time, God allowed something great to happen. Eddie's dad asked God to come in his heart. He was saved. If this bad accident did not happen, I truly believe Eddie's dad would not have had the opportunity to see firsthand how God works. Praise God!

My family and I have witnessed to many people. We have told our story to unbelievers and believers. We have seen the works of God firsthand. We have seen God raise the dead (me), heal the blind (Robyn), heal the deaf (Eddie), heal the lame (Eddie, Robyn, and me), and have had unbelievers accept God into their hearts.

We are human, and I would not be telling the truth if I said that we don't worry, question, and sometimes doubt things will be okay. But because of what we went through, we know God will not forsake us. The disabilities and scars we have remind us that scars are not injuries. A scar is a healing after injury; a scar is what makes you whole. So praise God we don't have to hide scars.

Because of what we have endured, our children are able to witness to others. They have told our story to their friends and have asked them to not drink and drive. We have seen many people saved. I read something very true on someone's Facebook account the other day, and it reminded me of how precious our God is. This is what I read:

> Last evening, as I prepared for bed, I happened to look at my then-shirtless body in the bedroom dresser mirror. My wife was passing by at that moment and I said, "Baby, I'm so sorry my body has so many scars." She didn't bat an eye, but instantly replied, "Jesus had scars, too." Now, I'm no Jesus, not even close, but if scars were good enough for Him, they are certainly good enough for one as lowly as I.

That precious person also said, "Friend, don't allow your scars to remind you of their pain in being created, or their often-awful costs. Let your scars remind you of what God has seen you through and what Christ endured for you."

So when I look in the mirror and see my not-so-perfect face and body, Eddie's face and body, and Robyn's face and body, I now can smile and feel blessed because without the scars and memories, my family and I would not have truly seen and been a part of God's works.

After reading about my family's journey, I hope that it will touch someone's heart and give them courage to be strong and never give up on everyday trials. God has plans and a purpose in everyone's life. He is the Alpha and Omega, the Beginning and the End. No one should ever try to go through life without God.

Day 11

Faith Brings Surety

And without faith it is impossible to please him,
for whoever would draw near to God must believe
that he exists and that he rewards those who seek
him.

—Hebrews 11:6 (ESV)

Yesterday we talked about three of the seven things that faith in God will always do. This morning we will talk about the last four. We found that *faith will always lead to salvation, faith will always defend us, and faith will always provide.* We must realize that it is impossible to please God without walking in faith. The truth of it all is that God rewards those who seek Him, and the only way to truly seek Him is to walk by faith. Therefore, let's learn to walk more closely to God by understanding clearly the last four things that faith will do.

Faith will always place us on solid ground. "Believe in the Lord your God, so you will be established" (2 Chron. 20:20). Only faith in the one true God (Father, Son, and Holy Spirit) places us on solid ground. Any other source of faith is shaky ground, sinking sand, and is unreliable. The old hymn says, "My hope is built on nothing less than Jesus blood and righteousness; I dare not trust the sweetest frame, but wholly lean on Jesus name. On Christ the solid rock I stand; all other ground is sinking sand, all other ground is sinking sand." Jesus must be always be the object of/for our faith, trust, belief, and total reliance. Any other foundation besides Jesus is sinking sand.

Faith will always add surety to our prayers. "This is the confidence that we have in Him, that if we ask anything according to His will, He hears us" (1 John 5:14). Possibly the greatest failure that exists within the church today is our lack of faith that is clearly demonstrated in our prayer life. Time and time again, God continues to prove His willingness and ability to provide and answer our prayers. That is whatever we ask according to His Will and in His Name. We are much like the children of Israel. We continue on our own journey, in our own ignorant ways, running around in circles like chickens with our heads cut off because we do not trust God. We have stopped listening for God's voice and instead grumble and complain that God isn't listening and He isn't doing what we want when we want, so we had to go back into slavery rather than walk by faith. They had forgotten that Moses prayed and asked God to part the sea, and God heard and He answered; Joshua prayed for the sun to stand still, and God heard and He answered; David prayed that God would take care of Goliath, and God heard and He answered. So with a sling and five smooth stones, God through David dropped that ten-foot giant to his knees.

We must realize that faith lives in folded hands and bent knees. Faith thrives in humility and surrender. The faith that moves mountains is filtered through a prayer life that has obediently taken up his/her cross and is following Jesus. The prayers of a faithful man or woman will shake the world. A power-filled life has never been a case of sleight of hand. A faithful power-packed life has always been the result of the confident prayer life of God's people.

Faith will bring power and strength to the family. "The house of the wicked will be overthrown, but the house of the upright shall flourish" (Prov. 14:11)

No other physical institution is as important to the church today as that of the home. There is no greater debate today than the one over the home. Satan knows that the best way to destroy the witness of the church is to destroy the home. So we see that debate plastered everywhere. Satan, the "deceiver" and "father of lies," is leading the great debates that are destroying our homes. The issues are too numerous to discuss, but there is no doubt that Satan is attacking the institution of family by beginning with the deceptions within the institution of marriage. The divorce rate is at its highest. Dysfunctional marriages and families have become the norm. The problem is that we as the church have brought these debates into our gathering as His church. The truth is that there shouldn't even be a debate. The truth of God's word is not debatable. Faith in God and wholehearted obedience to His word is the only source for truth, and only faith will bring power and strength back into our homes.

As Christians, we should be the greatest example for those in the world to follow. The world does not need to hear our debates; they need to see Jesus in us, in our homes, in our marriages, and through our lives. When the family fails, it is not God's fault. All our problems begin when we take our eyes off Jesus and begin debating God's truth with Satan's lies. Instead of praying with our mate, we try to answer the problems of marriage with our own understanding instead of following God's principles of commitment and fidelity that are found in His Word. When will the family be saved? When the children of God get the intestinal fortitude to say it is *my* fault, *my* sin, *my* neglect, *my* avoidance of issues, and *my* refusal to live according to God's Word and allow God to fill the voids in our marriages, families, and lives. Let's quit pointing the fingers and blaming someone else and take a stand for our family's sake by walking by faith.

Faith will move mountains and slay giants! "Jesus said to them, 'Because of your little faith. For truly, I say to you, if you have faith like a grain of mustard seed, you will say to this mountain, "Move from here to there," and it will move, and nothing will be impossible for you'" (Matt. 17:20).

It doesn't take a lot of faith to make us powerful through God. It simply takes God to make us powerful through faith. David had enough faith in God that he took five stones to defeat a giant. Don't miss the truth that only one stone was for Goliath, and the other stones were for each of his sons. "These four were born to the giant in Gath, and they fell by the hand of David and by the hand of his servants" (2 Sam. 21:22).

> Lord, may we walk faithfully with You and for You today. Let us discover today that our faith in You alone will move mountains, will bring power and strength to the family, will always add surety to our prayers, will always place us on solid ground, will always lead to salvation, will always defend us, will always provide, and will move mountains and slay giants. Amen.

Day 12

Walking by Faith Means Following, No Matter the Cost

As they were going along the road, someone
said to him, "I will follow you wherever you go."
And Jesus said to him, "Foxes have holes, and
birds of the air have nests, but the Son of Man
has nowhere to lay his head." To another he said,
"Follow me." But he said, "Lord, let me first go and
bury my father." And Jesus said to him, "Leave the
dead to bury their own dead. But as for you, go and
proclaim the kingdom of God." Yet another said, "I
will follow you, Lord, but let me first say farewell
to those at my home." Jesus said to him, "No one
who puts his hand to the plow and looks back is fit
for the kingdom of God

—Luke 9:57–62 (ESV)

We have already discussed the truth that God has provided everything necessary to live the godly life. Jesus is all we need. Jesus breathes life into us, giving us the provider of life—the Holy Spirit. It is true we have everything that we will ever need living inside us when we have Jesus. But most importantly, when He has us. When we are living as though we have tapped into His eternal provision and when we forsake our attempts at narcissistic substitutes, then we will be taking the next step in walking by faith.

Let's take a look at the cost of following Jesus. Did you realize that there is a cost to following Jesus? There is, and we count that cost each and every time we make a decision in our life. It is true; every time we make a choice, we either determine that the price is too high to go there or disobey, or we count the cost adequately and make the choice to follow Him, therefore walking by faith.

What is it going to cost us to follow Jesus? The flippant answer is everything, but that is the off-the-cuff answer, and we only say that so quickly because we have not adequately counted the cost. Don't get me wrong, everything is the correct answer, but everything to most of us is simply saying, "I give him my whole life." We throw the word *everything* out there so quickly because we have not followed Him with the reckless abandon that He requires in the past. Putting it bluntly, giving Him everything to us has become merely giving Jesus lip service. So let's truly count the cost.

What does it cost us if we don't follow Jesus? It will cost us eternal life, abundant life, our guidance in this life. We won't ever know the truth, and we will never be able to obey and glorify God. In essence, summing it up quickly, not following Jesus will cost us everything.

In learning to adequately count the cost, we will begin in Luke 9 and move to Luke 14, but before we do, we must realize that anything that competes with Christ for our loyalty must be forsaken as an idol. That is why Jesus said in Luke 9:23, "If anyone would come after me [follow me], let him deny himself and take up his cross daily and follow me."

Luke 9 gives us an account of three men whom Jesus met as He travelled along with His disciples. Two of these men had said that they wanted to follow Jesus and to become one of His disciples. The other guy was one who Jesus summoned to come and follow Him. For this lesson, let's just look at how Jesus dealt with these inquirers. While we try to recruit as many people as we can to follow us, our church, or our ministry, Jesus handled things a little differently. He seems to spend a great deal of His time telling these men why following Him is not such a good idea when looking from the outside in. Jesus was not looking for a crowd, but instead He was looking for sold-out followers who would walk by faith. Therefore, His dissuasive speech was to weed out the uncommitted.

Our commitment cannot be based on what we get, but solely on what we give, and we are to give it all. A servant's heart is what Jesus is looking for in us. Jesus was attempting to weed out casual Christianity. Why? Because as a follower of Christ, we have no earthly security.

The first guy made the same bold statement that many of us have made. "I will follow you *wherever* you go!" How can we even say then when we don't even know where Jesus is leading? When we don't even know what may be involved in the journey? Jesus is saying following him will take wholehearted commitment and unconditional surrender, so we need to know what we will have to give before we just flippantly throw out an answer like that.

So Jesus replies and says, "Hey, it will not be an easy road where I am going." He says, "Foxes have holes, and birds have nests, but the Son of man has nowhere to lay His head." In other words, Jesus has no earthly security. He was loaned accommodations to stay by those who loved Him, and he even borrowed a coin to tell a story. If you remember, Jesus even borrowed a donkey to ride into Jerusalem and fulfill the prophecy. If we can't remember that, Jesus was even buried in a borrowed tomb! (It was just as well because He didn't need it for long!) Jesus was saying that there is no security in things!

Jesus wants us to know that those who choose to truly follow Him must be prepared to go down the same road He went down. Followers of Jesus walk by faith because they have no earthly security. The only security a follower of Christ has is found in the faithfulness of God and a life beyond this one, and nothing can take these away!

> Lord, Your word this morning is hard to swallow because far too many of us have found our security in earthly possessions. Help us, oh Lord, to abandon it all and truly follow You! Amen.

Day 13

Walking by Faith Leads to Complete Security

> As they were going along the road, someone
> said to him, "I will follow you wherever you go."
> And Jesus said to him, "Foxes have holes, and
> birds of the air have nests, but the Son of Man
> has nowhere to lay his head." To another he said,
> "Follow me." But he said, "Lord, let me first go and
> bury my father." And Jesus said to him, "Leave the
> dead to bury their own dead. But as for you, go and
> proclaim the kingdom of God." Yet another said, "I
> will follow you, Lord, but let me first say farewell
> to those at my home." Jesus said to him, "No one
> who puts his hand to the plow and looks back is fit
> for the kingdom of God."
>
> —Luke 9:57–62 (ESV)

The follower of Jesus will walk by faith, and they will seek to further their walk with Jesus daily, but to do so they must adequately count the cost. Believing will only become faith when we are walking in obedience. Make no mistake, it is not your own doing! "For by grace you have been saved through faith. And this is not your own doing; it is the gift of God" (Eph. 2:8). Remember, 2 Peter 1:3 says, "His divine power has granted to us all things that pertain to life and godliness."

We have to realize that as a follower of the Savior, we have *no* security in this world, and for those who have simply believed and have not started following, or those who followed for a while but got off track, if you're going to follow Jesus and walk by faith with Him as he requires, then it may well cost you everything!

Here is the thing. Some of us have surely counted the cost, but our count was inaccurate. Some have falsely believed that as long as they have just enough of Jesus for fire insurance (to keep them out of hell), then that is all that they need. According to Matthew 7: 21–21, "Not everyone who says to me, 'Lord, Lord,' will enter the kingdom of heaven, but the one who does the will of my Father who is in heaven. On that day many will say to me, 'Lord, Lord, did we not prophesy in your name, and cast out demons in your name, and do many mighty works in your name?' And then will I declare to them, 'I never knew you; depart from me, you workers of lawlessness.'"

Jesus is saying to us right now that our calculations are way off. He is saying that we have done as the three guys in Luke 9 and responded. The first guy said, "I will follow you wherever you go" (Luke 9:57–58), but we can't give up our earthly security long enough to get around to actually following Him, and after counting the cost, we settle for knowing who Jesus is instead of following, and so our response since that day is the same as the rich young ruler's response in Matthew 19:16–22: "Good Teacher, what good thing shall I do that I may have eternal life?"

So Jesus says to us, "Why do you call Me good? No one is good but One, that is, God." (In other words, if you recognized me for who I am, you would give it all up and follow me.) "But if you want to enter into life, keep the commandments."

We say to Him, "Which ones?"

And, Jesus said, "You shall not murder, You shall not commit adultery, You shall not steal, You shall not bear false witness, Honor your father and your mother, and You shall love your neighbor as yourself."

And we say, "Lord, we pretty much have those whooped!"

And Jesus says, "If you want to be perfect, go, sell what you have and give to the poor, and you will have treasure in heaven; and come, follow Me."

And we put our heads down and say, "Lord, my security is in this world" and turn away and keep living life the way we always have. Some are saying, "I may not be following God right now, but I have never said my security is in this world, or I can't follow you!" While it's true we might not have responded this way with our lips, we have responded this way with our hearts and actions. We have said this with our lack of obedience.

Or we respond like the second guy, "Lord, let me first go and bury my father" (Luke 9:59–60). In other words, we say, "Lord, I have got a few things to do first and then I will follow You or when I get time I promise I will follow You." But we never get around to following Him. The cost of giving up our time or trusting Him in every circumstance is just too high a price to pay. So we settle for attempting to line things out on our own, and we never make time to follow Jesus. We just get too busy.

We may even respond like the third guy in Luke 9:61–62, "I will follow you, Lord, but let me first say farewell to those at my home." In today's world, what we might say is, "Lord, let me go back to what I have always done for a little while, and I promise that I will follow you as soon as I sort some things out."

As the church, we say, "Lord, we are going back to doing what we have always done for a while, and then we will follow you later once we get comfortable again." Jesus says to us, "No one who puts his hand to the plow and looks back is fit for the kingdom of God." The follower of Jesus is only moving one direction, and that is vertically toward Him. If God says change it this way, we obey because it is what God calls us to, not what we know to be true, right, or the way it's always been.

When Jesus came, he was upsetting all the Jewish people because He was basically attacking the way they had always believed that things should be done, carried out, or situated. However, they were not looking at the scripture laid out by God, but their own interpretation of it. They were not allowing God to lead them to Him. They followed their own mantra and interpretation before they ever dug into God's word. One of the best quotes from a recent movie was this: "Only real risk reveals the quality of one's belief [faith]."

Lord, Help us to recognize where we have counted the cost incorrectly in our lives. And, Lord, help us to give it all over to You and wholeheartedly follow You. Amen.

Day 14
Walking by Faith Leads to Obedience

Now great crowds accompanied him, and he turned and said to them, "If anyone comes to me and does not hate his own father and mother and wife and children and brothers and sisters, yes, and even his own life, he cannot be my disciple. Whoever does not bear his own cross and come after me cannot be my disciple. For which of you, desiring to build a tower, does not first sit down and count the cost, whether he has enough to complete it? Otherwise, when he has laid a foundation and is not able to finish, all who see it begin to mock him, saying, 'This man began to build and was not able to finish.' Or what king, going out to encounter another king in war, will not sit down first and deliberate whether he is able with ten thousand to meet him who comes against him with twenty thousand? And if not, while the other is yet a great way off, he sends a delegation and asks for terms of peace. So therefore, any one of you who does not renounce all that he has cannot be my disciple." (Luke 14:25-33, ESV)

Salt without Taste Is Worthless

Salt is good, but if salt has lost its taste, how shall its saltiness be restored? It is of no use either for

the soil or for the manure pile. It is thrown away.
He who has ears to hear, let him hear.

—Luke 14:25–35 (esv)

It is not totally the individual believer's fault that they have simply believed, never moved to obedience, and never followed to become a disciple because we as the church have been focused far too long on making converts and growing numbers when Jesus's commission requires that we make disciples and disciple makers. Too many local churches' response to Jesus has been at least "We are leading people to believe," "We just need numbers," or "We are too comfortable where we are to follow what Jesus requires." These are all narcissistic responses to Jesus, and as a result, we are not doing as well as we think we are at fulfilling "the Great Commission."

The reality is that we have not led others to become disciples and then disciple makers because we ourselves have settled for resting in the comfort of our belief. That was exactly the case of the religious leader of Jesus's day. So we will understand is that Jesus is not impressed with religion. There is simply no heart in religion itself. As the church, we must realize that to God, people are not simply a number, and God isn't impressed with our religious attempts. God is not interested in how many people we have led to come to church and simply believe. He requires that we lead them to be disciples, obedient followers, and disciple makers. As individuals, we must realize simply believing is not what is required. Faith is what is required, and faith involves trusting, believing, obeying, and following. James 2: 19 says, "You believe that God is one; you do well. Even the demons believe—and shudder!"

When we have adequately counted the cost, what Jesus said is planted permanently in our heart: *"Whoever walks by faith, follows and loses his life for My sake will find it!"* Whatever we think we are giving up for Christ, whatever price we feel like we are paying, and whatever we have sacrificed to follow Jesus is not a loss at all. Everything that we give up, we are actually giving over to Jesus and allowing Him to breathe life into constantly.

Therefore, the disciple or follower of Christ has no earthly ties because our ties are only eternal, and since Jesus is the only Way to eternity, we are completely tied to Him. But just when we think we have grasped the fact that Jesus requires that we give Him everything we find, what Jesus says in Luke 14: "If anyone comes to me and does not hate his own father and mother and wife and children and brothers and sisters, yes, and even his own life, he cannot be my disciple."

Most believers never walk by faith and truly follow Jesus because they don't clearly grasp the fact that our love for Jesus is to be so strong and so dominant that in comparison to our love for our mom, dad, wife, children, brothers and sisters, and even ourselves looks like hate. These words are hard when we look at it from the standpoint that we are hating the ones we love, but that is not the case at all. We love them enough to give them over to Jesus and follow Him, no matter what it costs.

Too many of us don't want to bear our own cross and are still waiting for someone else to do it so we never walk by faith. "Whoever does not bear his own cross and come after me cannot be my disciple" (Luke 14:27, ESV) Luke 9:23 tells us that we are to "deny our self and take up our cross daily and follow Jesus."

So we have to count the cost all over again. In fact, we are to daily and decision by decision count the cost to following Jesus. We can only adequately count the cost when we deny our self, take up our cross, and put to death anything that may keep us from wholeheartedly following Him, no matter what it costs. "For which of you, desiring to build a tower, does not first sit down and count the cost" (Luke 14:28, ESV)

What does Jesus tell us it costs to follow Him? *Everything!* "So therefore, any one of you who does not renounce all that he has cannot be my disciple" (Luke 14:33) Why? Because the follower of Christ not only has no earthly ties, but the follower of Christ can have no earthly distraction.

Not walking by faith and not following Jesus results in us losing our flavor as Christians. "Salt is good, but if salt has lost its taste, how shall its saltiness be restored? It is of no use either for the soil or for the manure pile. It is thrown away. He who has ears to hear, let him hear" (Luke 14:33, ESV). That is what has happened in too many lives and too many local churches. We have lost our flavor.

The great news is that when we love Him with everything we have, then His love is able to filter through us in such a way that we actually love others the way we should. Therefore, what we give up is not actually giving anything up, but instead giving everything up and trusting Jesus with everything and allowing Him to filter out the things that hinder our walk with Him, and should we compare our love for our family to our love for Him, we should love Him so much that it looks like hate in comparison.

> Lord, help us to wholeheartedly follow You. I know that we won't until we properly count the cost, oh Lord. Lord, it is so clear that You want us to count the cost because following You requires that we have no earthly ties and no earthly distraction, and that truth is made right in our lives, then we will be walking by faith.

Day 15

Faith Is the Pursuit of Righteousness

His divine power has granted to us all things
that pertain to life and godliness, through the
knowledge of him who called us to his own glory
and excellence, by which he has granted to us his
precious and very great promises, so that through
them you may become partakers of the divine
nature, having escaped from the corruption that
is in the world because of sinful desire. For this
very reason, make every effort to supplement your
faith with virtue, and virtue with knowledge, and
knowledge with self-control, and self-control with
steadfastness, and steadfastness with godliness,
and godliness with brotherly affection, and
brotherly affection with love. For if these qualities
are yours and are increasing, they keep you from
being ineffective or unfruitful in the knowledge
of our Lord Jesus Christ. For whoever lacks these
qualities is so nearsighted that he is blind, having
forgotten that he was cleansed from his former
sins. Therefore, brothers, be all the more diligent
to confirm your calling and election, for if you
practice these qualities you will never fall. For in
this way there will be richly provided for you an
entrance into the eternal kingdom of our Lord and
Savior Jesus Christ. Therefore I intend always to
remind you of these qualities, though you know

them and are established in the truth that you
have. I think it right, as long as I am in this body,
to stir you up by way of reminder, since I know
that the putting off of my body will be soon, as our
Lord Jesus Christ made clear to me. And I will
make every effort so that after my departure you
may be able at any time to recall these things.

—2 Pet. 1:3–15 (ESV)

There is great news today! Our perfect, complete, righteous, holy, and Almighty God has provided everything that we will ever need to live the Christian life. That is not just good news for us as individual believers, but it is good news for us as His church. You and I should be shouting His praises from the highest mountains, from the lowest valleys, and all along the way for He alone is the provider, protector, and power for living.

Second Peter 1:3–4 reminds us that God alone gives us everything that we need to live the life that He has called us to live. We talked a little about how He does it. We talked about why we have stopped or slowed down in our walk of faith. We found that we only have power as long as we have the breath of life being breathed in us by Jesus. Jesus is the Way, the Truth, and the Life. Since our sin knocked the breath of life out of us in similar fashion to Genesis 2, Jesus breathed life back into us as we were saved and given hope and a brand-new life through His death, burial, and resurrection. That life that He breathed into us is the Holy

Spirit. There is no life without the presence and power of the Holy Spirit in mankind.

No, anyone who does not have the Spirit does not have life. God fashioned us in such a way that we are made up of three parts (body, soul, and spirit), and the Spirit is the provider of and power for life. As a result, without the Spirit, we are without hope, destined for destruction, and without life.

We said the problem with many local churches, members, and Christians today is that they are lifeless because they have had the breath knocked out of them. Make no mistake, the truly saved are the truly saved and are sealed with the Spirit. Their names are written in the Lamb's book of life, and they have eternal life, but many still live a lifeless and powerless life. Why? Because they have had the breath knocked out of them. They are sealed with the Spirit, but they are not filled with the Spirit. They have drifted so far away from Jesus that they no longer have the breath of life being breathed into them. They have lost their luster, shine, and flavor for God.

When we are truly denying ourselves, taking up our cross, and following Jesus in wholehearted obedience, then we are abiding in the vine, and Jesus continues to breathe the breath of life into us, therefore producing good fruit through us. I believe that this is critical to being in the world, but not of the world (Rom. 12:2 and John 17:16). It is the key to walking by faith.

When we are abiding in Jesus, He is breathing the breath of life into us, and we are walking by faith. When we are truly walking by faith, we are living as though we are in the world, but are not of the world. To walk this way, we must practice listening to the Holy Spirit, allowing Him to powerfully live in and through us as our guide as He consistently and constantly leads us to Jesus so that Jesus can breathe more life into us. Then we have

> escaped from the corruption that is in the world because of sinful desire. For this very reason, make every effort to supplement your faith with virtue, and virtue with knowledge, and knowledge with self-control, and self-control with steadfastness, and steadfastness with godliness, and godliness with brotherly affection, and brotherly affection with love. For if these qualities are yours and are increasing, they keep you from being ineffective or unfruitful in the knowledge of our Lord Jesus Christ. For whoever lacks these qualities is so nearsighted that he is blind, having forgotten that he was cleansed from his former sins. Therefore, brothers, be all the more diligent to confirm your calling and election, for if you practice these qualities you will never fall. (2 Pet. 1:5–7)

Hearing what the Holy Spirit says to us takes practice, but if we are to live the life that He wants us to with the power that we should, then we must practice. Make no mistake, the Holy Spirit's number one job is to lead you and me to Jesus.

> Lord, help us to learn to hear what Your Spirit is saying to us, where He is leading, and where He wants us to go. Of course, Lord, we know Your Spirit is leading us to gain new and fresh revelations about Your Son Jesus. Leading us to become ever more intimate in our relationship with You. Have Your way today, and help us to practice hearing and obeying Your every word. Amen.

4

Faith Is Confidently Trusting

In chapter 2, Derrick shared his testimony of faith and how God is daily changing his life in such a way that Derrick's faith has become one-directional. In this chapter, Meagan, Derrick's wife, will discuss how her faith has taken her from the point of giving up to confidently trusting the Lord. It has been amazing to see firsthand what God is doing in Derrick and Meagan's walk, including their life, family, and marriage.

Meagan's Story

Meagan tells her story this way.

> I was raised in a Christian home where my dad is a deacon and my mom is a Sunday school teacher. This has been the truth all of my life. As long as I can remember, my family has always been members of one of two local Baptist churches. As is stated, my

daddy is an ordained deacon, and my mother either worked in the nursery or taught Sunday school to the little ones. I remember that I would frequently help her teach from my middle school years until my first year of college.

At the age of seven, I began to truly grasp all the Bible stories that I was taught. It was around that age that my granddaddy, my father's daddy, one of my two favorite men, lost his battle with cancer. I remember attending his funeral and thinking to myself, *I want to be in heaven with him too when I pass away.* I told my mom about it, and my mom began counseling me. She wanted to make sure that I knew in my heart what it meant for Jesus to die on the cross for my sins. I also remember thinking to myself, *Jesus died, Granddaddy died, but when Jesus died, He was beaten and put on the cross to die.* I remember feeling so sad about Jesus's death and began to wonder how that could have happened for me, and the seriousness and reality of death sank deeply within my heart.

Make no mistake, I knew what it meant to be religious and to be a Christian as I grew up in the church. We would regularly attend mass every Wednesday and Sunday and many other times that the doors were opened. In fact, I would bet that if the doors were open, we were there!

The two main Baptist churches in our town had incredible youth groups. Our town might have had a small school, but these churches had large youth groups. Therefore, the cool thing to do was to be a part of one of the two youth groups. So that is what I did, and my freshman year in high school, our youth group attended a youth conference in Dallas, Texas. At that time I heard the Lord's call and felt Him calling me to get involved in some sort of counseling ministry for girls my age or even in the middle school age group.

When the conference was over, I came home and told my parents, and we were all excited about God's calling. Over the next few years, my faith continued to grow, and I remained very active in the youth group.

Things began to change the summer before my senior year as a very good friend passed away in a tragic motorcycle accident. It devastated me. I had a very difficult time even dealing with it, and death seemed to rear its ugly head in my life once again. It wasn't that I questioned God. I knew He was in control and that He knew what He is doing. I just did not understand. The truth is, I was taught to never question what God does, so maybe that was why I didn't question Him, but no matter how hard I tried, I just couldn't wrap my head around it.

It was not long after that when I started hanging out with people outside the church. These new friends were from the same school that I attended, and they loved to drink and party. Of course, at that point, my best friends from church no longer wanted to be my friends because if they hung around me, then it would be considered guilt on their part by association. At almost the same time, my parents, for certain reasons, decided to move our membership to the other Baptist church in our town. So even though I was still around my peers in this new youth group, I wasn't around the friends that I had grown up with. For me, at that stage of my life, it was literally like moving from one clique to another, except in this case, the newer clique was not very inviting and even less accepting of me.

After graduation, I began simply working and attending college. My first year I attended a local college, and my second year I simply had to get away and moved to an out-of-town community college to put some distance between me and my former life. I really just needed a change and a different setting.

The new college that I attended seemed takes me even further away from whom I knew I should be as the cool thing to do was drink, and the even cooler thing to do was to smoke pot. Drinking and smoking had become a lifestyle for me at this point in my life, and by the end of my second semester, that was all that I seemed to do. I still managed to pass all my classes, and because they were all mini semesters, I was able to finish and return home by the week of spring break. Nevertheless, I was still trying to drink and smoke whenever I could.

During that time, I got reacquainted with a very close friend that I had not seen in a long time. It was nice to just catch up and reconnected. While at home, I decided to move back, and about a month after I moved home, I met my future husband, Derrick. After a couple of months, we became inseparable. I remember telling my dad, "I didn't know this was how I was supposed to be treated, and I didn't know I could be this happy."

Around this same time, death would soon rear its ugly head in my life again. A short time after Derrick and I started to get close, I received a phone call from the friend that I had recently reconnected with, only to tell me he loved me and thanked me for always being a good friend to him. Just three days after that call, I found out that he and another guy were in a tragic car accident so bad that their bodies could not be identified. I thought to myself, *The Lord giveth, and the Lord taketh away.* Again death had caught me off guard, and I was completely traumatized. This time death would lead to a completely downward spiral in my life.

For the next four years, my life and Derrick's would be completely consumed with drinking and smoking. We basically worked to pay bills and feed our habit. It wasn't until we found out about or first child, our baby girl, Brylie Grace, that our habits would change at all. Brylie seemed to change our lives completely, at least for a little while. We would still drink every now and then, but nothing like before, but after our second child, Brody, was around a year old, those old habits crept back into our lives.

At this point, Derrick and I were miserable in our marriage. In fact, saying that we could hardly stand to be around each other would be an understatement. We never talked to one another. In fact, we would only text to talk about the babies. It wasn't long before our drinking and smoking had taken over again. The only difference was this time, we were doing so more frequently just to stand being around one another.

All the while, my best friend who was a young mother who had a girl almost the same age as Brylie and was the most influential person at this point in my life was about to face tragedy. She was a single mother, about my age, with a hard-core faith in Jesus Christ. She was an amazing friend. On day as she and her daughter were alone in their apartment, she suffered a horrible asthma attack. Amazingly enough, her parents seemed to come to check on her at just the right time, but while at the hospital, she went in a coma. I was horrified by the possibility of one of my friends facing death once again. Within an hour, my friend's brain had developed calcifications, which meant there were no brain waves. About an hour later, the doctors took her off life support. Again, "the Lord giveth, and the Lord taketh away." Needless to say, I was traumatized.

Finally, on August 2013, I had had enough. I was at an all-time low. My marriage was all but dead, my friends were dying right and left, and my life seemed pointless. Satan had taken such a foothold on me that he had convinced me that everyone would be better off without me, especially my children. Depression had taken such a hold of me that I was literally at peace with myself not being around anymore. I figured that if I wasn't around, my kids would be better taken care of and better loved. After all, Derrick would finally be happy because he would no longer be stuck with me or stuck in a relationship that he didn't seem to want to be in.

Things had gotten so bad, and my depression had progressed to the point that two days earlier, I had gone to the doctor and was prescribed medication for severe depression.

The third day of August, I let Satan completely in, and I could not take life any longer. I had finally had enough, and I took over half my prescription of generic Xanax and chased it down with an insane amount of alcohol. I thought this was the solution to all life's problems, when actually it was my desperate cry for help. I ended up in the ICU for observation for one week. I had survived what could have easily taken my life.

Six months later, still fighting for our marriage, Derrick began going to church. He and my parents took our kids to church Sunday after Sunday. It wasn't until April that I returned to the church too. I rededicated my life to Christ, putting everything from the past in God's hands. I would now trust Him no matter what would come my way. I had finally realized that faith is trusting God in the good times and the hard times. Faith is confidently trusting God even when you can't understand why things happen the way they do.

As I completely laid my burdens at Jesus's feet, I began to be thankful for every blessing God had given me and my family. I began to be thankful for my marriage, for my kids, for my parents, being raised in church, but especially for the fact that Jesus died for me and was raised on the third day, and one day He is coming back for me. I no longer feared death, and I knew who to run to when Satan attacks.

The blessings just seemed to keep coming, or maybe I was now more aware of God's blessings. On May 14, 2014, my husband, Derrick, trusted Jesus, his Lord and Savior, and then on May 25, our first wedding anniversary, Derrick was baptized.

Derrick and I found our love for one another only after realizing God's love for us. We continue to grow in our marriage daily as we grow in our faith. We have become faithful only because God is faithful.

Derrick and Meagan actually only learned to walk by faith as they learned to walk with God, learned to walk to please God, and learned to count wholeheartedly on God. God continues to mold and align this young couple's life to His plans, His will, and to His Son's image as they learn to remain in Christ and follow Him with their lives and their family.

Day 16

Walking by Faith Is Walking with God

He walked with God.

—Genesis 5:24

Did you know that according to medical experts, walking is one of the most profitable forms of physical exercise? Walking stimulates the heart and lungs, strengthens the bones and the muscles, increases blood flow, and is one of the leading contributors to weight loss. Because walking is so good for us, we are encouraged to walk.

Did you know that the average pair of feet take seven thousand to eight thousand steps a day, about two and one-half million steps a year? In our lifetime, we will walk approximately 115,000 miles.

As amazing as that is, God wants us to understand that the Christian life is a walk that goes far beyond those 115,000 miles. In fact, it is a journey that goes beyond commitment, and it requires dedication, courage, and persistence. It calls for a totally surrendered life, a fully yielded life, and an intense desire to please God rather than ourselves. The spiritual walk that the Bible talks of is an active exercise of faith. Our success in completing this walk is not dependent upon our own natural or physical resources, but upon the strength, leadership, and controlling influence of the Holy Spirit.

When you talk about "a walk with God," Enoch should come straight to mind. He is one of two men of whom it is said, "He walked with God." He is one of two men who lived a complete life on this earth and went to heaven without passing through the portals of death. He is the only one, except our Lord and Savior, of whom it is written that "he pleased God." Why? Well, according to Genesis 5:24, "he walked with God."

How do we make sure we have a walk like that? We walk by faith. Our text says, "Enoch walked with God." Listen, this is not an ordinary walk, and we can't keep company with just anyone. We walk with God. However strange it may seem to our finite minds, it is possible, according to the Word of God, to live in the Spirit and walk in fellowship with the heavenly Father. Enoch's walk emphasizes an important relationship between humanity and divinity, between God and man, between the weak and limited and the all-powerful and unlimited. Think of the how great the privilege is that we have to walk with God.

Enoch knew the very character of God, and he walked with Him. In fact, there was never a time or a day when he did not walk with God. Can we walk like that? Yes, we can.

God said in Leviticus 26:3 and in 2 Corinthians 6:16, "If you walk in my statutes and keep my commandments, and do them; I will walk among you and will be your God, and you shall be my people."

And 1 John 1:7 says, "If we walk in the light, as he is in the light, we have fellowship one with another, and the blood of Jesus Christ his Son cleanses us from all sin."

True fellowship with God and true fellowship with one another is made possible only through Jesus Christ, God's Son. The walk the Bible speaks about means we have discovered the road of truth, and we know and trust the character of God. Jesus declares, "I am the Way, the Truth, and the Life. No man comes to the Father except by me." Some people say, "We need to be more open-minded. There are several roads that lead to heaven. You can go your way and I'll go mine, and we'll both get there."

Really? Jesus says He is the only way, so it is a one-way road, and he said it is a narrow gate; it has a straight way, and only a few will find it.

Others say, "Well, it doesn't really matter what you believe, so long as you are sincere in believing it." I beg your pardon! Sincerity is only a commendable trait as long as it is based on truth, and Jesus said He is the truth! I have absolutely no doubt that Adolf Hitler was a sincere man. He believed in what he was doing, saying, and sincerely sold a nation on it. Jim Jones with his cult in South America was as sincere as one could be, but his sincerity was not truth. He coaxed or forced nearly a thousand people to commit suicide in the name of religion.

So I am here to tell you today, right now, it does matter what you believe! What does your walk show? How are you living? Do we say that we believe God, yet live as if God doesn't exist? Are we practicing unbelief in our lives? If so, then we are not walking with God. If our conduct says otherwise, we are not walking with God. If we have the true faith of which the Bible describes, then we will place our total trust in God and see Him by faith and live accordingly. Our faith is built on nothing less than Jesus's blood and righteousness, and it must be lived out in faith and based on His character and truth. The psalmist says, "Teach me thy way, O Lord, I will walk in thy truth: unite my heart to fear thy name" (86:11).

Day 17

Walking by Faith Is Living to Please God

He pleased God.

—Hebrews 11:5

The Bible says that Enoch had this testimony that "he pleased God" (Hebrews 11:5). How was Enoch able to please God? The writer of Hebrews tells us that "without faith it is impossible to please [God]" (11:6). Enoch could walk with God because he was a man of faith and placed his trust in God. God is a big God. He is the God of the maximum and not the minimum, the God of might and miracles. He is the God of unlimited power, and He will always reveal Himself to us if we will believe and trust Him.

He will shake heaven and earth in order to reveal His glory and power to His people. In 2 Corinthians 3:5, Paul says "Not that we are sufficient of ourselves to think anything as of ourselves; but our sufficiency is of God." Paul never glories in the flesh but ascribes the winning of life's battles to "Him that loved us." Walking in faith means walking in God's power. His power is at work in us and through us and for us. Because this is true, our lives do not have to be sick and wishy-washy. We can be men and women of faith, enthusiastically aware of the adequacy of divine grace of God for our every need. Ephesians 1:19 states, "According to the working of his mighty power." And Romans 16:25 says, "To Him that is of power to establish you."

There are over fifty other passages that give us authority to "be strong in the Lord and in the power of his might." Walking by faith not only means finding adequacy only in Him; it also means growing in Christ. Colossians 2:6–7 shows, "As you have therefore received Christ Jesus the Lord, so walk in him, Rooted and built up in him and established in the faith, as you have been taught, abounding therein with thanksgiving." In this one passage, Paul talks about four elements of the Christian life: walking, growing, building, and abounding.

Walking expresses life. Growing expresses an inner power. Building up shows progress of character until God perfects His work in us, and abounding reflects the abundance of joy and a proper attitude for the marvelous benefits that walking with God gives to us along the way. The reason some people have so little joy in their Christian walk is that they are not following these four steps. As one preacher said about our walk, some people sit on it, soak in it, and some are sour about it.

The true Christlike life is a growing life. A walk of faith with God must be built downward, "rooted in Christ," built upward, "built up in him and established in the faith," and then abounding joy and thanksgiving become the results of this dynamic growth experience in our Lord Jesus Christ. When we walk with God by faith, we will experience intimate fellowship with Him. "What a fellowship, what a joy divine, Leaning on the everlasting arms…I have blessed peace, with my Lord so near, Leaning on the everlasting arms" (1887 Hymn "Leaning on the Everlasting Arms" by Anthony J. Showalter and Elisha Hoffman). We have discovered, as did Enoch, that walking and living in the presence of God is an experience of blessed fellowship and sweet communion. It is always a pleasant experience to walk with someone you love.

There are some wonderful things that God, our walking companion, does for us as we put our faith in Him. He guides us, He comforts us, and He protects us as we walk together. The psalmist wrote, "For this God is our God for ever and ever: he will be our guide even unto death" (Psalm 48:14). When we take this journey with our capable and trusted guide, we can leave our worries behind. He arranges all the details. He knows the destination because he has been there before; all we have to do is go with him, listen to him, place our faith in Him, and follow His instructions. We will never walk alone. He is with us. He reminds us, "They that wait upon the Lord shall renew their strength; they shall mount up with wings as eagles; they shall run and not be weary; and they shall walk, and not faint" (Isa. 40:31).

> Lord, Help us to Live in such a way that we are living to please You and You alone!

Day 18

Walking by Faith Aligns Us with God

"By faith Enoch was translated that
he should not see death."

—Hebrews 11:5

We read in Hebrews 11:5, "By faith Enoch was translated that he should not see death." The word translated is an old Latin word, which simply means "carried over" or "carried across." God carried Enoch across to the other side. Someone described it by saying, "One day Enoch and God were walking along, and God said to Enoch, 'Why don't you go home with Me today? You've been with me for 365 years.' So God carried him across—carried him across death."

Death is that force that divides this world from the world to come. God picked up Enoch and carried him across to the other shore. One moment walking with God in time, the next, in eternity. One moment, communing with God by faith, the next, by sight. Enoch's life of faith was at last crowned by an abundant entrance into the life of perfect fellowship.

We must learn to keep in stride with God. You see, the real test of our walk is in reality a test of our character. To see how it lines up with God's character. It is not what we do in the outstanding, exciting, on fire, and extraordinary places in our life that define us, but instead what we do in the mundane, everyday routine, running low on motivation and non-exciting times of our life that determine our walk. It is vital that we realize that it is in the atmosphere of constant fellowship with God that we learn the necessary truths for living a complete life. The walk we seek can never be found in and by our own intellectual reasoning. When we are in constant fellowship with God, the Holy Spirit transforms our perspective, and our impossibilities become possible in and through the Lord. When this happens, our lives are then molded by His character and His perspective as walk in stride with Him. It is He who is keeping us in stride as our fellowship becomes constant.

Just like Enoch, we must always live our life in such a way that we cultivate constant fellowship and a thriving relationship with God. Keep in mind that Enoch was not fellowshipping with God just on Sundays. In fact, it wasn't only on Sundays and Wednesdays. His fellowship with God was twenty-four hours a day, seven days a week. It wasn't on and off every other hour, day, month, or even every other year. Enoch walked with God constantly and lived a complete life.

> Thou hast a few names...which have not defiled their garments; and they shall walk with me in white: for they are worthy. He that overcomes, the same shall be clothed In white raiment, and I will not blot out his name out of the book of life, but I

will confess his name before my Father, and before his angels. (Rev. 3:4–5)

What a wonderful promise! We can walk with Him in white. White garments in heaven signify purity, perfection, and holiness. It doesn't matter whether it is a white robe or a three-piece white suit or a totally new design from heaven's wardrobe, the important thing is that we shall walk with God in everlasting perfection. Now we walk by faith, but then our eyes shall be open to the fullness of all His eternal wonders. Now we walk with limited understanding, but then life's most baffling mysteries will be resolved in the light of His eternal wisdom. Yes, this walk with God leads home. Let's be sure that we daily "walk worthy of God, who hath called you unto his kingdom and glory" (1 Thess. 2:12).

> Lord, help us to keep in step with You. And, Lord, may we never get ahead of You, and may we never stray too far behind. Amen.

Day 19

Faith Counts on God

Because of the LORD's great love we are not
consumed, for his compassions [mercies] never
fail. They are new every morning; great is your
faithfulness.

—Lamentations 3:22–23 (NIV)

Most of us wake up each day to the same old routine. There
are usually no surprises and nothing new. It is just the same
routine day in and day out.

But that is not the case for what God has prepares for
us. He prepares for us daily something special. His mercies
or compassions for us are new every day, and they never fail.

Aren't you glad you don't just get one dose of mercy for
life? Aren't you glad that God is moved with compassion
daily for our sake? It is "because of the LORD's great love
we are not consumed, for his compassions [mercies] never
fail." If He wasn't moved by His great love to give us a
daily dose of His compassion and mercy, then we would
simply be consumed because of our sin. But we can count
on Him every single day to reach out in His great love with
a compassion that never fails and with a compassion that
is brand-new.

God proves His faithfulness to us every single day
with His great love. The word *great* comes from a Hebrew

word meaning "manifold or multiplied by myriads." In other words, God's love provides to us new mercies every morning because His faithfulness is manifold and multiplied by myriads.

Paul said it this way, "Now to him who is able to do immeasurably more than all we ask or imagine" (Eph. 3:20. It's His exceedingly immeasurable greatness that makes new mercies available to us every single day. Yes, even when we have failed Him in the most miserable way. God is faithful! *We can always count on God!* That just feels good to say. We need someone we can count on. Have you ever thought you trusted someone, and then by the end of the day, you don't know if you can depend on anyone to keep their word or promises?

God is not and never will be one of those people. *He will always be faithful*. He will do what he said He would do. He will keep His promises. He will always be there for you. He only speaks truth. We never have to guess whether or not God's Word will be fulfilled. We know it will because He is faithful. We never have to worry about being defeated because He has already won the victory! But when we do mess up, we can know that he will be moved by His love with compassion to forgive us, love us, and lead us.

God wants to make us into someone who can be counted on. He wants to make us faithful. But we get so off track sometimes trying to be good-enough people and trying to be religious enough on our own, but God created us for something different and something more. He created us for a relationship with Him through His Son Jesus Christ. And guess what? God will never fail you with His part of that relationship. God is there no matter what you might do to compromise that relationship. "He will never leave nor forsake you."

Will you allow God to continue to make you into someone who can be counted on? God is faithful to do His part. Will you do yours? Will you trust His faithfulness? *We can always count on God!*

> Lord Help us to be faithful because we can always depend on You to be faithful. Amen.

Day 20
Faith Won't Be Lost

On that day, when evening had come, he said to
them, "Let us go across to the other side." And
leaving the crowd, they took him with them in the
boat, just as he was. And other boats were with
him. And a great windstorm arose, and the waves
were breaking into the boat, so that the boat was
already filling. But he was in the stern, asleep on
the cushion. And they woke him and said to him,
"Teacher, do you not care that we are perishing?"
And he awoke and rebuked the wind and said to
the sea, "Peace! Be still!" And the wind ceased, and
there was a great calm. He said to them, "Why are
you so afraid? Have you still no faith?" And they
were filled with great fear and said to one another,
"Who then is this, that even the wind and the sea
obey him?"

—Mark 4:35–41 (ESV)

Many people are scared to death in this life because their
faith is less than sustaining. In other words, somewhere
along the way in the journey of life, they have lost faith. For
the child of God, fear is simply an opportunity for faith, but
what often happens is that we place our trust in something
or someone other than God. From the very moment we
place our confidence in something or someone other than

the Lord, our confidence soon turns to worry or stress (a lack of or loss of faith). Our confidence, faith, and trust must always remain in and be directed toward God.

We should always respond in faith every single time trouble or distress comes our way. Faith is always the answer to our every fear and struggle. When fear assails and doubt arises (at that very moment), Jesus puts His finger on our spot of fear or struggle and says, "I want you to trust me right here!"

That is where we find the disciples. Jesus is pointing at their fear and their situation, and He is asking, "Where is your faith?" Their faith had taken a temporary leave of absence. Have you ever found yourself in the same situation? They had forgotten all the things Jesus had taught them and shared with them. Jesus told them not to worry because He would take care of them in every situation, and all they need to do is trust Him (Matt. 6:30).

Today, Jesus is pointing to our fears and our situations, and He is reminding us of this same promise. Jesus is saying don't lose faith right here or right here or right there. Right in the middle of our desperate struggles and scary situations, Jesus wants you and me to trust Him to take care of us. In reality, He is the only One who can.

Think about it! Jesus was right there with them. He was in the boat with them. Just a reminder: Jesus is always in the boat with us too! But their faith could not see past the facts and the reality of the situation. Remember it was storming, the weather was rough, and the seas were in chaos. The situation was impossible! Have you ever felt that way? Sure you have, but we must realize that true faith is not based on the facts or reality of our situations. True faith is based solely and fully on truth (who Jesus is and what He can and will do)! The sum of every fact added up to the fact that they were in trouble, but the truth was in the boat with them, and they did not recognize Him. Jesus is the Creator who has control and power over all creation. Jesus was and is always in complete control of every situation. He is sovereign. It is true, even when all the facts seem to be stacked against us, Jesus remains in complete control. The truth was that the One who came to bring life and life more abundantly was being overshadowed by a fear of the facts: the winds, the rain, and the unsettled seas.

What is prevailing in your life, a fear of the Lord, or a fear of the facts or situation? How do you react when things look bleak and the facts are stacked against you? Do you act like someone who has no hope? Do you seek the truth and allow God to be all that He has promised in your life? As believers, we will either trust God or lose heart and sink in an ocean of worry and distress. How do you think the disciples would have acted had they not lost faith?

The truth is, it is impossible for the boat to sink when the Master is on board! The storms of life will never wipe us out, and they won't last forever, but the peace and joy that Jesus brings during them will! James said, "Count it all joy, my brothers, when you meet trials of various kinds, for you know that the testing of your faith produces steadfastness. And let steadfastness have its full effect, that you may be perfect and complete, lacking in nothing" (James 1:2–4, ESV).

It is not that we are to be joyful because of the storms. We are to be joyful in the middle of them because Jesus is with us, and He is in control. We will consider it all joy when we truly realize that Jesus is always in control. God is always faithful, and it is impossible to lose faith when our faith is steadfast in the Master because He is greater than any fear. Make it your aim today to never lose faith, but instead to always hold on to Jesus.

> Jesus, help us to truly hold on to You because You alone are our future and our hope. May we never lose faith in You, Lord. Amen.

Faith Is Confidently Increasing

When we are truly walking by faith, our faith will be constantly and consistently on the increase. We may feel at times that we have been stretched like a rubber band, but as we are stretched by the faith, we will never be the same again. God is always at work, and he is always looking to stretch our faith as He grows us and the Holy Spirit shapes us to look a little more like Jesus every single day.

James and Tracy's Story

My friend James shares a story about a faith that is confidently increasing.

> My wife Tracy and I will be married five years this coming October. When we married in 2010, Tracy was a Texas realtor, and I was a tank welder working in chemical plants. We been raised in church and were both saved during grade school,

but during these days I'd refer to our spiritual state as "lukewarm Christians" at best. We had big plans and big dreams, and I can honestly say that being ministers didn't fit into our accomplishing those plans. Although we had both talked about maybe having callings upon our lives to work with youth someday, we had allowed the devil to feed us lies that God could never use us in those ways, that we weren't good enough.

My job caused us to travel all over the United States our first year of marriage. Then God blessed us with our little Ellie, who recently turned three in January 2015. Tracy and I continued traveling until August 2013, when God's call hit us like a ton of bricks. We were in Clarksville, Indiana, and I had been welding in a plant there for about a month. This had to have been one of the most difficult trips that we had ever been on. At the least, we can say that it had been different than our other trips. We had been watching as God began weaving strings of mercy into every aspect of our lives. We were both feeling more convicted than we ever had in our lives. We were mainly convicted that we were only living for ourselves and not for God.

One evening as I came home from work, I felt this heavy burden on my heart. So I just went into the bedroom to be alone with God. That night I shared with Tracy that God had told me to quit everything and go home and work with the youth. As I explained, I couldn't hold back my tears. I was scared to death because I didn't know where we would teach, how we would teach, how we would pay our bills, or any of the details. God had simply said, "It's time to go home and get to work!"

I had no idea how Tracy would react, but little did I know, God had already been working on her heart as well. In fact, she just didn't know how to share it with me. Tracy was in full agreement. We knew that our home was paid for, God had already blessed us with that, and we decided it didn't matter if we lost everything else. We wanted to live for His glory and not simply retire one day.

The next morning we packed the camper, and I called to explain everything to my boss. I apologized for leaving him in the middle of the job, and we then headed for home. I'd like to tell you that the two-day drive was easy, but Satan definitely tried to stop us. It took us five days to get home. It amazes me how quickly Satan attacks the instant we appear on his radar. When we were living for ourselves, Satan left us alone for the most part. Though we had an empty void from not being fully surrendered to God, the devil left us alone, but the very second that we decided to come home to minister to the youth, we immediately stepped onto a spiritual battlefield.

The first thing that Satan threw our way was that our camper caught fire while driving down the interstate. Next, our roadside service did nothing to help us. Then we were stuck at a gas station in one-hundred-degree weather, and we almost got the camper towed once we found a hotel. To top it all off, we couldn't find the part we needed to fix our broke-in-half axle. Let's just say we did a lot of praying! Satan's attacks had failed, though, because everything that had happened had made us even more determined to do what God wanted us to do. It was definitely a confirmation that the devil wasn't happy about it either.

Once we reached home nearly a week later, Tracy's father, who attended our home church, said that our new pastor, Brother Teddy Ott, had approached him the following week and said that he was excited to talk to us about the youth. We were dumbfounded; we hadn't told anyone that we had decided to come home to minister, but God had already prepared the way for our ministry. We met with Brother Teddy and his wife and shared our hearts. We were nervous and had no idea what we were doing, but we were just honest and shared that we had a hunger and a burden for the youth.

I'll never forget the verse God gave Tracy and I before our meeting that afternoon: "Do not be afraid or discouraged because of this vast multitude. For the battle is not yours but God's" (2 Chron. 20:15). Our Father God is so encouraging! When we are shaking like a leaf and we are so uncertain of the future, He lifts us up and encourages us and increases our faith. When He does, then we realize that all we need to do is give Him our hands and our hearts and allow Him to use us as he wants. God simply wants a willing vessel.

We were voted in as youth directors the first of that September 2013 by a 100 percent vote. That year was incredible. God grew the youth group from four students to twenty-five students. SWAG Youth Ministries saw twenty-six salvations and rededications. I was licensed as a pastor on July 6, 2014. Tracy and I were scared that we wouldn't be strong enough or have enough knowledge to teach and lead the youth, but God used us in a mighty way. He grew us so that we could help grow them. We shared our hearts, and there were struggles during that year. Satan wasn't done, but neither was God!

Our pay was cut at least three-fourths, we encountered a miscarriage with our second child, and great spiritual warfare was going on within the church. In spite of all that, it was the most amazing year of our lives. The youth became our kids, and their struggles became our struggles. Most of all, God became number one in our lives, our marriage, our home, and our future.

In August 2014, God began talking to Tracy and I once again, but this time it was about resigning from the church. What? How could this be, God? So for months, God had been leading us to move north to Kilgore, Texas, to further our ministry. Two weeks into August, just one week after vacation and spending some much-needed time alone with the Lord, we gave the church our resignation. We shared with them that we didn't have a church to minister in and that God was simply telling us once again to go and have faith.

Again our faith would be ever increasing as God was sending us on another adventure. Many in the church didn't understand. They would reply, "How you could leave your youth group to move somewhere where you have nowhere to minister?" Tracy and I had begun to trust God so fully with our lives that we would go to the moon if He said that is where He wanted us and if there were lives that He needed to help save there.

Leaving our youth group was one of the hardest things we have encountered so far, but we know that there is a perfect reason to why God wanted us to move to Kilgore. We have now been living in Kilgore, Texas, continuing to grow in our faith and relationship with the Lord. He continues to prepare us spiritually for what lies ahead as we wait, watch, and listen for the next step He wants us to take.

When we realize how much God loves us, yearns for our attention, and cares for us, we will follow Him anywhere, and our faith will increase with every step. We must understand that it's not just simple right-and-wrong choices when it comes to picking up our cross. It is about building a relationship with our Father; our wants become His wants, and our hands become His hands. We will be walking by faith when we are denying our self and taking up our cross and following Him. We will notice the increase in our faith as denying our self and taking up our cross becomes instinct in our everyday life. God wants us to love serving Him, and not simply follow Him because we are afraid of Him or for the "fire insurance" that He can give.

God wants our walk to be a life-changing walk, one that prepares us for eternity. God wants our walk to be a lifelong relationship with Him. Our God is an awesome, loving God who wants to make sure that we don't go through the journey of life without completely experiencing His awesomeness or His love in complete faith.

Day 21

Faith Is Staying Confident

O Lord, thou hast searched me, and known me....
Search me, O God, and know my heart: try me,
and know my thoughts.

—Psalm 139:1, 23

I don't know about you, but there have been times in my life when I didn't want God to know my heart or my thoughts. Most people feel that their heart is okay. Sure, there are times when they get a little angry, greedy, irritated, or self-consumed, but overall, their heart is good. We also feel that our thoughts aren't as bad as someone else's. How we know that, I have no idea because I have never been a mind reader, but nevertheless, we typically rationalize that way.

There is no typical day when we ask God to search us and know us. On a typical day, we are too busy hiding our thoughts from God to allow Him to search us. Besides, if we took the time to let Him search us, then what He found might interfere with our plans or the temporal pleasures we seek. He might want us to change something! It is so vital to our daily walk and life for us to seek the Lord and ask the Him to search us and try us.

We need to know where we stand with the Lord. We need to know the vast distance between our thoughts and His thoughts. We need God's loving correction. We need to know whether or not our thoughts are glorifying God or not. We need to know if our heart is in the right place. We need to know if our heart is filled with His love or not. We need to know if our motives are right or if we need God to change them. We need God to direct our path that we need to follow, but we won't when we refuse to let Him search us and know us. It is for our benefit, but also for His glory when we do. Everything we do is to be out of love and for the glory of God.

It is true, Paul said, "Whether you eat or drink, or whatever you do, do all to the glory of God" (1 Cor. 10:31).

We need to know when our thoughts have swallowed us up and we have become self-seeking. James said, "If you have bitter envy and self-seeking in your hearts, do not boast and lie against the truth." This wisdom does not descend from above, but is earthly, sensual, and demonic. For where envy and self-seeking exist, confusion and every evil thing are there. But the wisdom that is from above is first pure, then peaceable, gentle, willing to yield, full of mercy and good fruits, without partiality, and without hypocrisy (James 3:14).

We need to know daily if we are seeking the Lord in all the events of our day, or if we were seeking our own desires. We have a tendency to be self-seeking and to hide that truth by hiding our heart and our thoughts. To the Colossians, Paul says, "And whatever you do in word or deed, do all in the name of the Lord Jesus, giving thanks to God the Father through Him" (Col. 3:17).

We need to know if we have offered thanks and given God the glory for everything or when that has been replaced by our patting our self on the back. Our hearts and thoughts must be wholeheartedly His so that we "rejoice always, pray without ceasing, *in everything give thanks*; for this is the will of God in Christ Jesus for you. Do not quench the Spirit. Do not despise prophecies. *Test all things*; hold fast what is good. Abstain from every form of evil" (1 Thess. 5:16). We need to know from the Lord the truth of our thoughts and what is filling our heart. We need to know that there is a melody of delight flowing from our heart purely for God.

Will you allow the Lord to search you and know you today? I pray that you will because that is the only way we can remain in Him and glorify Him with all that we are! Lord, will you search me and know me right here, right now, today?

> Lord, may we become more confident as we ask You to search us and know us so that as we know ourselves, we can move ever closer to You!

Day 22

Letting God Fog-Proof Our Faith

What shall I do with you, O Ephraim? What
shall I do with you, O Judah? Your love is like a
morning cloud, like the dew that goes early away.

—Hosea 6:4 (ESV)

If you live in East Texas, then you know about early
morning fog. It doesn't matter what time of year it is; you
never know when you will have a foggy start. The faith of
many believers starts off each morning the same way (with
a foggy start), but for many, their faith never gets any better.

How do we know? Our verse this morning says, "Your
love is like a morning cloud, like the dew that goes early
away." Have you ever noticed that you start off the day
loving everyone, but at the end of the day, you don't even
like anybody? This is a devastating place to be for the
believer because it is a sign that we have a foggy faith. But
what does it mean to have a foggy faith? A foggy faith is
often followed by an empty or fleeing commitment to the
Lord. It looks like this: We start off our walk with God
with a strong commitment, and we get up early in the
morning and begin every morning with quiet time, but the
moment time becomes an issue or when almost any other
conflict arises, our loyalty to God takes a backseat. When
it does, we begin roaming around aimlessly in life, looking

for answers in all the wrong places, and begin settling for temporal treasure to get us by. Therefore, it doesn't take long before we become so distraught and stressed out that we can't see God through the fog.

It is true; it seems as though He speaks to us less, answers our prayers less, and some of us even get to the point where we have talked ourselves into believing that God cares about us less. At the very least, our faith has become so foggy that we live as though God doesn't care about the details of our life. There are others of us whose faith has become foggy due to the fact that they have served Him with their lips for so long that they simply stopped being His hands and feet.

When our service to the Lord, commitment, and walk with the Lord become overshadowed by the fog of a shaky faith, we stop loving, serving, and trusting the Lord the way we should. It is almost as if as soon as our feelings of devotion and service to Him fades, so goes our faith in Him. That should not be the case. We are to love Him with all our heart, all our soul, all our mind, and all of our strength. We must not simply talk a good talk, but we must walk a good walk. God will never evaluate our faith on what we say it is or base on how well we fake it and go through the motions. No, God evaluates our faith on what lasts—the truth in our hearts. For this reason, the word of God (the truth) will either be the death of the sin or the sinner.

What happens when we drive into a fog? Well, the first thing that happens is that we can't see very far ahead or us.

The same is true spiritually. We have a foggy faith when our faith is based on seeing with the physical eye. We must have a faith so grounded in God that whether our physical eyes can see or not; our spiritual eyes can see Him just fine. Fog often creeps in without us realizing that it is coming. Therefore, we must make sure that our faith is fog-proof. We must make sure that the clouds of doubt, worry, stress, and distress are not determining our faith, but instead our faith is burning through those clouds.

Fog is made up of condensed water droplets, which is the result of the air being cooled to the point (actually, the dew point) where it can no longer hold all the water vapor it contains. The same is true with our faith. It can become so cooled off by the droplets of discouragement, doubt, and disappointment that our faith can no longer hold all the droplets it has bottled up. As a result, our faith becomes foggy.

When we remember God is faithful (Hebrews 10:23), not to forsake the assembling (Hebrews 10:25), and be patient and hang in there (Hebrew 10:36) and set our sights on pleasing God (Hebrews 11:6), then we are on track to overcoming a foggy faith. When things aren't going our way, we must remember He is able! Let's make sure that we aren't walking a walk or living a life that has become blinded by a foggy faith.

Lord, we ask that You protect us from a foggy faith, but if and when our fog does become foggy, help us to recognize it quickly and allow You to deal with it diligently.

Day 23

Seven Things to Make Your Faith Grow

Let your roots grow down into him, and let your
lives be built on him. Then your faith will grow
strong in the truth you were taught, and you will
overflow with thankfulness.

—Colossians 2:7 (NLT)

Thousands of books have been written on faith and hundreds of thousands of sermons and millions of words discuss faith, yet God stirred me to write seven things to make your faith grow. So growing our faith is an ongoing project, one that never ends. Faith is like a seed, plant it in your heart and your mind. At the appointed time, God will give you a mega harvest of what you need just when you need it. How do you grow strong in faith? Well, it's a process.

Here are the seven things to make your faith grow.

1. Feed your faith with the Word.
   "Faith begins where the will of God is known."
   How do you know the will of God? Read your Bible.
   Begin doing what it says, and you will have a growth
   spurt in faith. Psalm 34:8 says, "O taste and see that
   the Lord is good: blessed is the man that trusteth
   in him." The Message Bible translation says, "Open
   your mouth and taste, open your eyes and see—

how good God is. Blessed are you who run to him."
Psalm 119:103 in the Message says, "Your words are
so choice, so tasty; I prefer them to the best home
cooking. With your instruction, I understand life."

By feeding on the Word, you never have to wonder or worry about what to do next. The Word of
God is alive. It is like food that nourishes our souls.
Our faith activates the Word. John 14:26 says, "But
the Helper, the Holy Spirit, whom the Father will
send in My name, He will teach you all things, and
bring to your remembrance all things that I said to
you." Reading the Word allows the Holy Spirit to
bring to our remembrance exactly what we need to
apply to our daily situations.

2. Exercise your faith by your actions
   In the same way, faith by itself, if it is not accompanied by action, is dead (James 2:17). At some point,
   our faith must become action. If it doesn't, then
   there is no evidence of faith at all.

3. Speak in faith to make it grow.
   I love preaching in churches where the people
   speak back to me. I'm reminded of a story I heard
   once about a preacher who had a congregation that
   would talk back to him during his sermon as they
   got excited about their future. One Sunday morn-

ing, the preacher said, "This church is like a crippled man who needs to get up and walk under the power of Jesus." The congregation replied with enthusiasm, "Let it walk, preacher, let it walk." Then the preacher said, "This church, like Elijah on Mount Carmel, has got to run." The congregation replied with enthusiasm, "Let it run, preacher, let it run." Then the preacher said, "This church has got to mount up on wings like eagles and fly." The congregation replied with enthusiasm, "Let it fly, preacher, let it fly." Then the preacher added, "Now if this church is going to fly, it's going to take *money*." The congregation replied with lack of enthusiasm, "Let it walk, preacher, let it walk."

That's not exactly what I would call speaking your faith. Second Corinthians 4:13 says, "I spoke because I believed." In the same spirit of faith, we also speak because we believe. There are also times when you will speak about things of faith before they ever manifest in the natural realm. Your boldness in your faith will open doors of opportunity for you. First Timothy 3:13 says, "Those helpers who do their work well win for themselves a good standing and are able to speak boldly about their faith in Christ Jesus."

4. Free your faith from negativity.

    "Feed your faith and starve your doubts." The word *negative* isn't really in the King James Version of the Bible. However, when I think about the word *negative,* I'm reminded of the word *doubt.* Someone once said, "Faith and doubt cannot live in the same house" (James 1:6). When doubt leaves your life, you are presented with unlimited opportunities. Matthew 21:21 in the New Living Translation says, "Then Jesus told them, 'I tell you the truth, if you have faith and don't doubt, you can do things like this and much more. You can even say to this mountain, "May you be lifted up and thrown into the sea," and it will happen.'"

    How do you get rid of doubt or negativity? James 4:7 says, "Submit yourselves therefore to God. Resist the devil, and he will flee from you."

    Someone once said, "You get faith by studying the Word. Study that Word until something in you 'knows that you know' and that you do not just hope that you know." John 10:17 in the New King James Version says, "So then faith comes by hearing, and hearing by the word of God."

Read your Bible. Believe what it says.

> Lord, help us to be intentional with our faith by reading, studying, and obeying Your every Word. Amen.

Day 24

Seven Things to Make Your Faith Grow (Continued)

Let your roots grow down into him, and let your
lives be built on him. Then your faith will grow
strong in the truth you were taught, and you will
overflow with thankfulness.

—Colossians 2:7 (NLT)

Let's continue with our list.

5. Believing the impossible as possible.
    Luke 1:37 says, "For with God nothing is ever
    impossible and no word from God shall be without
    power or impossible of fulfillment."

    With God, nothing is impossible. Well, there
    is one thing: it's impossible to please God without
    faith. Hebrews 11:6 says, "But without faith it is
    impossible to please him: for he that cometh to God
    must believe that he is, and that he is a rewarder of
    them that diligently seek him."

    According to the Greek, the word for *rewarder* is
    misthapodotēs, and it means "one who pays wages, a
    rewarder." He is one who pays wages to those who
    diligently seek him. Are you getting this? Jeremiah
    17:10 says, "But I, the Lord, search all hearts and
    examine secret motives. I give all people their due

rewards, according to what their actions deserve." What are your due rewards for diligently faithfully seeking him? You're going to get paid for it.

6. Sharing Jesus with others.

    Do you want to know how you can understand and receive every blessing God has for you? The answer is found in Philemon 1:6: "As you share the faith you have in common with others, I pray that you may come to have a complete knowledge of every blessing we have in Christ." Every blessing we have in Christ.

    First Chronicles 16:8 says, "Give thanks unto the LORD, call upon his name, make known his deeds among the people."

    When we're recognized in our jobs, we want to tell all our friends about it. When we're selected for special recognition at church or in any sort of activity, we want to let people know about it. When our children excel in a sporting event, academics, or extra-curricular pursuits, we like bragging about them.

    Why, we even brag about our pets for doing a particularly good trick, our cars for their gas mileage or how they look, our big-screen TV...the list could go on. There is nothing wrong about the various scenarios listed, unless we testify about everybody or everything else except for the greatness of God. The question each of us need to answer is, how much time do we spend bragging about our God, the one who woke us up this morning, clothed us in a right mind, and gave us air to breathe and food to eat? The scripture is very clear. We're to tell the world "who the Lord is and what He's done."

Psalm 34:3 says, "O magnify the LORD with me, and let us exalt his name together." One more scripture. Colossians 3:15–17 in the Message Bible says,

> Let the peace of Christ keep you in tune with each other, in step with each other. None of this going off and doing your own thing. And cultivate thankfulness. Let the Word of Christ—the Message—have the run of the house. Give it plenty of room in your lives. Instruct and direct one another using good common sense. And sing, sing your hearts out to God! Let every detail in your lives—words, actions, whatever—be done in the name of the Master, Jesus, thanking God the Father every step of the way.

We thank Him is by doing what He says in His word. Share your faith.

7. Discussing our faith frequently with our Manufacturer.

   Our manufacturer created an instruction manual for each of us to survive and thrive in any and every situation, circumstance, and problem we face in life. Here's a revelation: if we don't read and study it, then we'll continually have problems all the days of our natural-born life. Second Timothy 3:16-17 says, "All scripture is given by inspiration of God, and is profitable for doctrine, for reproof, for correction, for instruction in righteousness: That the man of God may be perfect, thoroughly furnished unto all good works."

   If something is profitable, it's going to be beneficial. The word *profitable* in *Strong's Concordance* is from a Greek word that means "profitable, advantage." If we want to have advantages in life, then we need to understand our instruction manual—God's Holy Word. Every answer to every problem we face is in the Bible.

   "Faith is believing that God is going to take you places before you even get there." "Your belief determines your action and your action determines your results, but first you have to believe." "Fear looks; faith jumps. Faith never fails to obtain its object. One pastor said, "If I leave you as I found you, I am not God's channel. I am not here to entertain you, but to get you to the place where you can laugh at the impossible."

Now it's time for you and me to take God's Word and read and begin to make our faith grow stronger than it's ever been.

> Lord, help us to commit to growing in our
> faith each and every day!

Day 25

Putting Faith into Practice

Therefore, my beloved, as you have always obeyed,
so now, not only as in my presence but much more
in my absence, work out your own salvation with
fear and trembling, for it is God who works in you,
both to will and to work for his good pleasure

—Philippians 2:12–13

The first step in growing spiritually is maintaining a desire to grow. Jesus said, "Blessed are those who hunger and thirst for righteousness, for they shall be filled." We will never grow spiritually until we have the desire to grow spiritually.

Next, we must move from a desire to grow to "maintaining the right diet for growth." Remember, we need a steady diet of "spiritual food" that only comes from God's Word. We said though we don't miss many physical meals, we live as though it is not a problem to skip spiritual meals. Just as a child cannot grow physically without the proper diet, neither can a child of God grow spiritually without the proper diet of His word. Jesus said we can't "live by bread alone, but by every word that comes from the mouth of God." He didn't say by listening to His word; he said by living by His word. And since that is true, we need practice. Remember, growing is a process, and because it is, we must take one step at a time and must never stop. The process for growing is reciprocal, meaning the steps don't end, and once we come to the final step, we are to begin again with the first.

The third step in growing spiritually is that we must "exercise our faith and His word into practice." Exercise and practice are essential for physical development. If we were to ask any heart specialist about the two vital keys to a healthy heart, the reply would be "proper diet and regular exercise." The Great Physician tells us the same is true for being a "healthy child of God." Every student, athlete, musician, and disciple must realize that the right diet, exercise, and practice are needed to improve their skills or, in the case of the believer, to strengthen their walk.

Developing skills requires continual practice, as does following Jesus. We must learn to hear His voice, live by His word, obey His every command, and follow Him wherever He leads. Exercise and practice are critical to playing music, throwing pitches, shooting baskets, and following Jesus. Athletes run, lift weights, and practice for hours a day so that they can grow stronger, wiser, and develop endurance. It is like a child learning to walk; they will never learn without exercise and practice. This is true for any good student. Exercise and practice are essential to spiritual growth (Heb. 5:14). Those who are of full age, by reason of use, have their senses exercised to discern both good and evil. Growth requires exercise as well as nourishment. In 1 Timothy 4:7, it says, "Exercise yourself toward godliness."

The child of God needs a strong commitment toward strengthening their faith. This is only accomplished by exercising and practicing our faith. We must make it a routine practice to never give up and to keep on trusting God, no matter our situation or circumstances. Yes, even when it is not politically correct, we must practice exercising our faith. We cannot ever give in or up on our faith in order to please others. We can't please God or get to know Him better without exercising our faith.

God is not pleased with a faith never put into practice. Hebrews 11:6 says, "Without faith, it is impossible to please Him, for he that cometh to God must believe, that He is and that he is Rewarder of them that diligently seek Him." He is the reward that we seek! Walking in faith pleases God, and since this is true, we must put into practice teaching our children to follow Jesus, to seek Him first, to never put anything before Him, and we must exercise these things with our own faith. We must put God's word into practice in our own lives and exercise our prayer life by making prayer a consistent and routine practice. We must make exercise our discipline and our faith in God by eliminating the excuses for not going to church, small groups, or Bible study. We exercise our faith by faithfully attending, worshipping, learning, and applying His word to our lives. We have no problem with leading ourselves or our families to attend and practice for hobbies, schoolwork, or sports, but when it comes to leading and teaching them to exercise their faith, we fail in this practice. There is no exercise more important and no practice more vital than the exercise and practice of putting God first!

We have to do as Jesus said, "seek first the kingdom of God and His righteousness" (Matt. 6:33). We aren't growing because we haven't allowed God to fuel in us the desire to grow. We are stalemate in our growth because we are choosing the wrong diet. We remain tired, weary, and worn out because we are choosing the wrong priority.

Here are seven keys to exercising your faith.

> First, what you do in life will be a reflection of what you've learned (John 8:38).
>
> Second, our greatest desire should be for our deeds to reflect His instructions. Psalm 119:5 in the New Living Translation says, "Oh, that my actions would consistently reflect your decrees!"
>
> Third, faith must be an action, or it will always be inactive. James 2:17 says, "So also faith, if it does not have works [deeds and actions of obedience to back it up], by itself is destitute of power [inoperative, dead]."
>
> Fourth, it's a team effort. Faith in knowing that God's Word is true and actions that unleash faith into the natural realm. James 2:22 in the New Living Translation says, "You see, his faith and his actions worked together. His actions made his faith complete."

Fifth, you will be rewarded for the actions you take and consequences when you don't. Proverbs 24:12 in the New Living Translation says, "Don't excuse yourself by saying, 'Look, we didn't know.' For God understands all hearts, and he sees you. He who guards your soul knows you knew. He will repay all people as their actions deserve."

Sixth, our commitment to bring glory and honor to His name will automatically bring success to ours. Proverbs 16:3 in the New Living Translation says, "Commit your actions to the LORD, and your plans will succeed."

Seventh, you'll be paid for your faithful actions. Revelation 22:12 says, "Behold, I am coming soon, and I shall bring My wages and rewards with Me, to repay and render to each one just what his own actions and his own work merit." Therefore, we fail to exercise and put our faith into practice. Will you take the next step and begin the right practice and exercise program today?

Lord, help us eat right and exercise our faith daily. Amen.

6

Faith Is Wholehearted Commitment

If there is one thing that must sink in, it is the truth that faith is a wholehearted commitment, which is exactly what Deuteronomy 6:1–25 (NLT) calls for as it says,

> These are the commands, decrees, and regulations that the Lord your God commanded me to teach you. You must obey them in the land you are about to enter and occupy, and you and your children and grandchildren must fear the Lord your God as long as you live. If you obey all his decrees and commands, you will enjoy a long life. Listen closely, Israel, and be careful to obey. Then all will go well with you, and you will have many children in the land flowing with milk and honey, just as the Lord, the God of your ancestors, promised you.
>
> Listen, O Israel! The Lord is our God, the Lord alone. And you must love the Lord your God with all your heart, all your soul, and all your strength.

And you must commit yourselves wholeheartedly to these commands that I am giving you today. Repeat them again and again to your children. Talk about them when you are at home and when you are on the road, when you are going to bed and when you are getting up. Tie them to your hands and wear them on your forehead as reminders. Write them on the doorposts of your house and on your gates.

The Lord your God will soon bring you into the land he swore to give you when he made a vow to your ancestors Abraham, Isaac, and Jacob. It is a land with large, prosperous cities that you did not build. The houses will be richly stocked with goods you did not produce. You will draw water from cisterns you did not dig, and you will eat from vineyards and olive trees you did not plant. When you have eaten your fill in this land, be careful not to forget the Lord, who rescued you from slavery in the land of Egypt. You must fear the Lord your God and serve him. When you take an oath, you must use only his name.

You must not worship any of the gods of neighboring nations, for the Lord your God, who lives among you, is a jealous God. His anger will flare up against you, and he will wipe you from the face of the earth. You must not test the Lord your God as you did when you complained at Massah. You must diligently obey the commands of the Lord your God—all the laws and decrees he has given you. Do what is right and good in the Lord's sight, so all will go well with you. Then you will enter and occupy the good land that the Lord swore to give your ancestors. You will drive out all the enemies living in the land, just as the Lord said you would.

In the future your children will ask you, "What is the meaning of these laws, decrees, and regulations that the Lord our God has commanded us to obey?"

Then you must tell them, "We were Pharaoh's slaves in Egypt, but the Lord brought us out of Egypt with his strong hand. The Lord did miraculous signs and wonders before our eyes, dealing terrifying blows against Egypt and Pharaoh and all his people. He brought us out of Egypt so he could give us this land he had sworn to give our ancestors. And the Lord our God commanded us to obey all these decrees and to fear him so he can continue to bless us and preserve our lives, as he has done to this day. For we will be counted as righteous when we obey all the commands the Lord our God has given us."

God calls us to a vibrant, growing life of faith.

Marshall's Story

Marshall tells his story. How has my faith grown? My faith has grown through personal observation and by using the brain God gave me. God loves all things called according to His purpose. When we are grounded in His way and believe this, nothing can totally shake us or even throw us off our game. I think. "Okay, God, what is this about?" I know I'll understand it better by and by.

I didn't grow up in a church, but my grandmother and grandfather were devout members of the Church of Christ. We couldn't figure out why they were always calling us "the little heathens." We found out later in life when I was twelve years that my daddy had been married before. We were written off as progeny of an illicit union. I don't remember Big Mama ever telling me about Jesus, and I was taught in school to believe in evolution. As I got older and heard about Jesus from neighbors, I began to question evolution and realized what a crock it is!

When I was twenty, God sent me my wife. She was raised in church and has been faithful to Christ her whole life. She went to church while I worked, and she put up with me for twenty-five years. I was prideful and tried to take care of everything myself; of course, I couldn't. So I got more and more frustrated, which translated into more and more meanness until she grew to hate me. As a result, we divorced. After we divorced, I spent the worst years of my life. However, by the grace of God, we remarried and moved to Burkeville, Texas. She worked to get me in church because she knew that may be the only way to save me, and that church took us in. God immediately went to work on me in that church. Brother Eddie Sunday was the right vessel God used to start. God uses whomever or whatever he wants. Even if we are not 100 percent walking in the perfect path to him, he will use those available to reach us for His cause. We just have to be willing.

Brother Eddie left as pastor, and Brother Fred Rainy and his wife Linda were sent to us to help us find a new pastor. That is when Brother Teddy and Kelly Ott came into our life, and God changed everything! This was perfect timing for me and my family. I had trusted Jesus as Lord and Savior, and we were growing spiritually. Teddy and Kelly had to leave the church unexpectedly due to health reasons and probably expected us to wig out, but we had grown to the point where we knew God knew what he was doing.

We had just returned from Brownsville with the disaster relief team and were continuing to walk by faith. My family was learning from the Bible like never before. I realized that family includes church family and friends. I was experiencing God through prayer like never before and learning every day that life is a journey, not an event. God was refining us through Sunday school lessons. I'm excited and scared, but I can't wait to see what is next. From experience, it will be totally unexpected. Look for his will and where God is working, and do your best to join him. All things work together for the good of those who love Christ Jesus and are called according to His purposes (Romans 8:28).

My Faith

What has grown my faith?

1. God's timing
2. Lessons meant just for me.

I was shown by example the way godly people accept God's will in their lives. The way Brother Teddy and Sister Kelly up and changed their lives to come and pastor our church. I saw firsthand the house and lifestyle they gave up. I saw them leave their friends and family to come to minister to people they did not know because God wanted them to. They suffered emotionally. Brother Teddy's mother passed away physically, and he battled severe asthma while he was with us.

With their example in front of me, how could I say no to anything and everything God asked of me? Go to RA camp with a bunch of kids, sure. Picture this! The last day of camp seemed like three weeks ago. A big room with 170 boys ages ten to fifteen. All the men were told to stand against the back wall. Ninety percent of the men were pastors, youth pastors, or deacons. Here I was, probably not the most qualified person there to minister to a new convert (at least in my mind). An altar call was given, and about seven boys went forward. After a brief counseling session in front, they were told to go to the back of the room and find a man to pray with and talk to them about their newfound faith. This kid named Caleb B. stood up, turned around, and walked past his pastor, his youth pastor, and several elders in his church, all the other men there, and came straight to me. I knew it when he turned around. I started praying to God to please give me the words to say. I got the message loud and clear; without a doubt, God was showing me that he will use who he wants to get a job done. He does not just use the most qualified available to Him. He qualifies those he calls to do his work no matter their qualification. He does the work; he just wants to hear, "Yes, Lord, use me."

So many times, so many lessons, some not so dramatic, but always right on time, right when I needed it.

Well, maybe one time just as dramatic. God asked me to go on a Baptist Disaster Relief Mission to Brownsville to run shower trailers and laundry trailers to bring relief and comfort to illegal aliens (children and moms) who had overwhelmed the border patrol station we were sent to. Again I was just a little player helping with a cause spearheaded by others. We had been studying in church about "being broken." I asked God when I prayed to help me understand it. I even asked him to make it simple and unmistakably clear what that meant. I got my wish.

One day, I was taking care of my half of a shower trailer. My job was to show boys where to shower, keep watch outside till they came out, and then to clean and disinfect each shower to get ready for the next person. One day, two boys ran out quickly, and I smelled the worst smell of my life. I went in to find a boy of about seven crying his heart out and coming out of the trailer. I ushered him out to the guy assigned to assist after the shower and went in to find diarrhea all over the walls, the floor, and the benches. I knew immediately without a doubt that God had shown me "brokenness." I was instantly reminded of the time when I was seven and had asked the teacher in my class at school to let me go to the bathroom twice. She refused. I had an accident in my pants. I was stinking in my pants in front of all my classmates and stayed in the bathroom for an hour all by myself, crying my eyes out while my mother was summoned to take care of me. I knew God was reminding me that this is what it is like to be broken.

I ran out to find the boy being consoled by members of my church. I grabbed him and hugged him. I told him everything was all right and that I loved him. I then went and cleaned up the mess and got it ready with no qualms. I was reminded that God sees our sin as being on us like our own filth. He cleans us up and forgives us and loves us. I was later asked to work with the kids in our church.

Soon after, I was made aware of an almost desperate need for bus drivers at our local school. I was made aware that it was a great way to get to know kids, their parents, and to know their needs. I knew how hard it was to get a license to drive a bus. The lines, the money, the time to study— I knew how backed up the offices are. I prayed to God that if that is where He wanted me to go at this time to help me with the process.

I never had to stand in a line. I was granted an early test drive. No doubt I got my license. The superintendent of the school had the route I was to take over because of the shortage of drivers. I rode with him one evening. He showed me a spot way down in a subdivision and said, "Show up here at six thirty, and a boy named Brandon will be here, and he will help you."

Monday I got to the bus barn and thought surely someone will ride with me. It was before daylight, and I passed up the road to the school because it was so foggy and I couldn't see it. I did a lot of praying. I drove through the fog, found the subdivision, and then found Brandon in pea soup fog. Not by my wits, but with God's help.

Change? I believe God is in the change business. If you are not growing, you are not on the straight and narrow path. Don't get comfortable...get *worried* if you are. God wants you out of your comfort zone. A pastor, Brother Van Lowe, said to me, "I can see you wanting to leave. If they aren't making you comfortable..." I said, "No, we are leaving because we don't want to be comfortable as the rest of this church is." God wants us to grow. I didn't know where we would end up; I only knew it would be where God wanted us to be.

There's an epidemic in this country and its churches. Their members are too comfortable and aren't growing. More harm is being done by Christians who have lost sight of the Great Commission and have grown comfortable in their walk than anything else. They go through the motions of "church" while losing sight of God's plan for them. They get bogged down and forget that as Brother Teddy always says, "It's all about the heart." It does not matter what you do in the name of Jesus if it is not done out of love and with the right motives and attitudes. We must make it all about God. It is all for his honor and glory, His desires, His goals, His plans, His priorities, and, not the least, His timing. His timing is always perfect. Most of the time we can't see till later, sometimes much later. But it always bears out time and again.

To me, one of the most fascinating things to see is God working. I love trying to figure out the whys and what fors. Most of the time it takes me a long time to figure out where He is going with something. Sometimes I never do, but I know it is for a reason and continue to trust Him and walk by faith.

Day 26

Developing a Continuing Faith

Then he said to them all: "Whoever wants to be
my disciple must deny themselves and take up
their cross daily and follow me."

—Luke 9:23

Therefore I tell you, whatever you ask for in prayer,
believe that you have received it, and it will be
yours.

—Mark 11:24

Walking by faith helps us recognize the truth that it is
time that you and I stop playing church and start being
the church. We have discussed the fact everyone born again
through the blood of the Savior Jesus Christ is the church.

As the church, we must grow in our faith. In other
words, if we are His, our faith must grow. "By their fruit you
will know," so there is no way that our faith won't continue
to grow. Who does God intend that we grow into? His
image and become His disciples. We must move beyond
simply believing to becoming and being His disciples and,
therefore, actually living the abundant life He calls us to live.

A true disciple is always willing to know Him better and
follow Him more every day. Therefore, a true disciple will
always seek Him first and abide His word. A true disciple

will be disciplined for godliness, will be committed and faithful lifetime learners, and a disciple has a wholehearted faith. A disciple is sold out and all in for Jesus. They have counted the cost and leave behind anything that may keep them from following Him with all their heart.

A true disciple has a continuing faith. It is not that a disciple never struggles with faith, but that a disciple knows the Author and Finisher of faith so well that they continue on with Him, allowing God to transform the struggle into a stronger faith. Jesus said, "Whoever wants to be my disciple must deny themselves."

It takes focusing on Him to deny ourselves. Everything must begin with prayer, and every prayer must begin with praise. Our focus must remain on God so that we have the strength, wisdom, and understanding to continue on the faith, pressing on toward the prize of knowing Him. So a true disciple's continuing faith leads them to continue in prayer. A continuing faith is a reciprocal faith. It begins with Him and ends with Him. Yes, disciples fall and falter, but they always keep their eyes on the master and move toward Him in faith because they know "whatever they ask for in prayer while continuing in faith it will be theirs."

A disciple is not self-seeking, but instead trusts the Lord for His provision. Because they realize He alone is sufficient. They know that God is always faithful, just, and knows exactly what is truly needed. A disciple has a continuing faith that leads them to deny themselves and put to death anything that may keep them from continuing on after Jesus.

Do you have a continuing faith? It is true that a continuing faith isn't what is necessary for salvation, but it is necessary to be a disciple, to live the abundant life He gives, and to become disciple makers. Will you continue on in the faith today, no matter what comes your way?

> Lord, may You develop a continuing faith in us. A faith that pushes on towards You no matter what comes our way. Lord help sot continue on towards You day by day. Amen.

Day 27

Faith Leads to Becoming Committed and Faithful Disciples

Not that I have already obtained all this, or have
already been made perfect, but I press on to take
hold of that for which Christ Jesus took hold of
me. Brothers, I do not consider myself yet to have
taken hold of it. But one thing I do: forgetting
what is behind and straining toward what is ahead,
I press on toward the goal to win the prize for
which God has called me heavenward in Christ
Jesus.

—Philippians 3:12–14

Once we as believers move from simply believing to becoming committed and faithful disciples, then we will be on our way to walking by faith. And as we learn to be His disciples, we ultimately make disciples. Hopefully by now, we have all realized that at the heart of discipleship is our right response to God's call upon our lives.

Discipleship is a matter of willingness. A willingness to become all that God wants us to be and to live the life He is calling us to live. Are you willing? I pray that you are!

So far we have talked about the first two marks of a true disciple. We have found that a true disciple always strives to abide in God's Word. Next, we found that His disciples are always being disciplined for godliness. And thirdly we find that a true disciple is a committed and faithful lifetime learner.

The Greek word for *disciple* is *mathetes*. *Mathetes* actually means "learner" or, more specifically, "disciplined learner." Disciples are disciplined learners who are committed to pursue God with a faithful heart and a teachable spirit.

Disciples are eager to go wherever Jesus leads, to hear what Jesus is saying, to receive everything that Jesus has to offer, and to put off anything that will hinder their following Him. You see, disciples don't sit on the bench; they are actively learning, following, and living for Jesus at all times.

Disciples trust Jesus and will follow Him wherever He leads. They come to Jesus with the heart and attitude that He alone is the One who can and will meet their every need. They trust Him as the One who will give them the rest they need in the middle of life's struggles, burdens, and demands (verse 28).

Disciples are willing to take Jesus's yoke upon themselves. They are eager to make His direction theirs and His priorities their priorities in life. They are eager to faithfully share in Jesus's life and His ministry (verse 29). They earnestly desire to learn from Jesus. In fact, disciples will arrange their entire lives around learning, growing, and being changed into the image of Jesus Christ every day (Matt. 11:28–30). Every disciple realizes that discipleship is a lifelong process (Phil. 3:12–14).

Disciples don't just learn from Jesus until they feel that they have learned enough to make it on their own. No, discipleship is not like going to high school or college where in four years we can graduate. Instead, being a disciple requires us to be committed and faithful lifetime learners. Why? Because we press on to take hold of that for which Christ Jesus took hold of us. We do not consider ourselves yet to have taken hold of it. But there is one thing we do: forgetting what is behind and straining toward what is ahead, we press on toward the goal to win the prize, which is to be Christlike. Oh, listen, we won't fully be the reflections of Jesus until we are "at home" with Jesus.

Disciples don't stop or slow down! They realize that they are preparing for Him and to go to the place that He went to prepare for them. A disciple always keeps moving in Jesus's direction and keeps learning from Jesus throughout their lifetime. As disciples, you and I are in the process of becoming like Jesus our Master. "When a disciple is fully trained he/she will be like their Master" (Luke 6:40). And every disciple will have the desire to be like the Master. Why? He is Life! He is everything, and they realize it!

Disciples constantly want more of Him and to be more like Him. And the more of Jesus they get and the more they learn from Jesus, the more their character, conduct, and commitments begin to reflect His character, His conduct, and His commitments (Eph. 4:13). "To put it clearly, being a disciple is a lifelong commitment to become like Jesus."

Disciples are committed and faithful lifetime learners because they want to look like the Master! How about you? Are you faithfully committed to Jesus to be a lifetime learner for Jesus?

> Lord, help us to realize that walking by faith will always lead us to be faithful and committed disciples as we are committed to become lifetime learners for the Kingdom's sake. Amen.

Day 28

We Need the Right Kind of Faith

And he [Jesus] said, "Truly I tell you, unless you
change and become like little children, you will
never enter the kingdom of heaven.

—Matthew 18:3

It is clear that faith is necessary for eternal life. "For by
grace you have been saved through faith" (Eph. 2:8). Not
only are we saved through faith, but it is impossible to
please God without faith. It pleases Him for the lost to be
found or for the perishing to be made alive. Over and over
in my heart, God continuously reminds me that He is not
willing that any should perish, and that He is waiting to
pour out His eternal grace on all who have faith. It does not
matter what I say or do in life outside of faith because it is
impossible to please Him at all without faith. "And without
faith it is impossible to please him, for whoever would draw
near to God must believe that he exists and that he rewards
those who seek him" (Heb. 11:6). It is clear that faith is a
necessity for life.

Especially the abundant life Jesus brings, but what is
faith? "Now faith is the assurance of things hoped for, the
conviction of things not seen" (Heb. 11:1). We all believe
in something, and what we believe in mostly comes from
the things we have witnessed to be true. Therefore, we only

believe in the tangible, and because we do, we have learned to how to doubt. Our doubting hearts and minds often cry out, "How is faith not in what is seen, I need proof!" As a result, we have become a skeptical and jaded people who try to rationalize and prove everything. The truth is that many believers never even know for sure as they hit their knees that God will actually hear their prayers or that He might actually answer them.

We have complicated faith to the point that we have forgotten what faith actually looks like. I am so thankful that because God knew we would try to complicate things, He provided all that is needed through His word to uncomplicated them. Jesus said, "Truly I tell you, unless you change and become like little children, you will never enter the kingdom of heaven" (Matt. 18:3). Here Jesus is painting the picture of what our faith is to look like. He said the perfect picture of faith is the faith of a little child. Keep in mind He is not saying a childish faith, but a childlike faith or a simple faith. There is a big difference between a childlike faith and a childish faith. A childish faith is one that is immature, floundering, selfish, and temporal at best, but a childlike faith accepts things in simplicity.

We often have a childish faith, and so we need to change our mind-set and our heart. Have you ever noticed that a child has a way of believing and trusting everything the parent says? It's only when we begin to grow up a bit that we tend to question everything. Someone once said that the "currency of heaven is faith." Faith is what pleases and moves God. So we need real faith, and it looks like the faith of a little child. When we are told to have the faith of a little child, Jesus is simply saying, "Completely trust in Me without condition."

Proverbs 3:5 commands us to "trust in the Lord with all your heart, and lean not on your own understanding and in all our ways acknowledge Him." The problem lies in the fact that we try to see faith through our own intellect and understanding, but that is not faith at all. Our faith is to be built on solid ground (the truth of God's word) and not our own perceptions. Jesus said in Matthew 11:25, "I praise you, Father, Lord of heaven and earth, because you have hidden these things from the wise and learned, and revealed them to little children." Here is the real key to the faith of a little child: little children are completely dependent on their parents for protection, nourishment, provision, guidance, the truth, and every necessity for life, just as we are to God. So here it is; we must have a faith that instinctively knows God, without hesitation responds to God, and spontaneously devoted to God. Real faith is a childlike faith. Will you come to Him as a little child today?

> Lord, help us to always have the right kind of faith.
> Help us to have a childlike faith. A faith where we
> trust You to meet our every need. Amen.

Day 29
What Good Is Faith Anyway?

What good is it, my brothers, if someone says he
has faith but does not have works? Can that faith
save him? If a brother or sister is poorly clothed and
lacking in daily food, and one of you says to them,
"Go in peace, be warmed and filled," without giving
them the things needed for the body, what good is
that? So also faith by itself, if it does not have works,
is dead....For as the body apart from the spirit is
dead, so also faith apart from works is dead.

—James 2: 14–17, 26

What good is it? What a great question for those who claim
to be faithful followers of our Savior! The Apostle John asks
a very similar question to this one used by the half brother
of Jesus. He asks, what do you do?

These are great questions that we can and should
use to help gauge our faith. We should always be about
reevaluating our faith. We should use questions like this
to pull that plumb line from faith to faith to see how we
align. Aligning our lives to Jesus is crucial to our faith. God
is always more concerned with our character (what we do)
than our comfort (who we think and say that we are). What
we do always reveals the truth of our character. For the
believer, character is vital. We have seen this in God's word
time and time again.

So let's ask ourselves the questions at hand and see how we line up. First John 3:17–18 asks, "What if you have enough money to live on [notice the question is not "if you were wealthy or had plenty," but just enough to live on] and you see that your brother or sister is in need of food and clothing, what do you do?"

God says that if you don't help him or her then, how can the love of God be in you? God then makes it clear that we are just to say, "Hey, I'll pray for you, everything will be okay." No, God says through this verse: "Let us not love with words or in talk only, but let us love by what we do and in truth."

We are sadly mistaken if we think that words bring the comfort and hope that people need and God wants. God wants us to share or demonstrate that we have faith. Faith and action go hand in hand. In fact, there is no faith without action. We cannot say we have faith in God if it is not demonstrated in the way we live. Our actions reflect the truth, no matter what we say. We can't just say we love other people and then treat them as an outcast.

Our faith is proved in how we treat other people. James's question in our verse today is "What good is it, my brothers, if someone says he has faith but does not have works? Can that faith save him? If a brother or sister is poorly clothed and lacking in daily food, and one of you says to them, 'Go in peace, be warmed and filled,' without giving them the things needed for the body, what good is that? So also faith by itself, if it does not have works, is dead."

When we see a need, we should meet that need by providing for the person. That demonstrates the truth of our faith. We can't turn our backs on people when they are in need. That doesn't demonstrate faith, but the opposite.

We need to always be willing put our faith into action. Faith and actions work together. There is a saying that goes "Actions speak louder than words." This is so true. We say we care all that we want to. We can even shout that we are faithful and that we love God and love others from the rooftops, but it means nothing if we don't back it up with actions. Faith is not a noun; faith is a verb. Faith is action, and so we must let the way we live show our faith.

> Lord, help us allow You to gauge our faith. Lord, we often need a clear, accurate picture of where we are in our walk with You. Lord, may our faith be demonstrated in all that we say and do!

Day 30

Faith Is Found in Total Surrender

And without faith it is impossible to please him, for
whoever would draw near to God must believe that
he exists and that he rewards those who seek him.

—Hebrews 11:6 (ESV)

For by grace you have been saved through faith.
And this is not your own doing; it is the gift of
God, not a result of works, so that no one may
boast. For we are his workmanship, created in
Christ Jesus for good works, which God prepared
beforehand, that we should walk in them.

—Ephesians 2:8–10 (ESV)

God is leading me to use two verses to help us understand
that we are left hopeless without faith. I praise God that
faith isn't something to gain, but instead is a gift that comes
with surrender. Why? Our verse makes it clear that "without
faith it is impossible to please" God. Notice the writer uses
the word *impossible*! In Greek, *impossible* is *adunatos*, which
means "unable" or "powerless." So in life, anything that we
do without faith is unstable, useless, or powerless.

So often we do what we are able, what we can see or do
in our own strength while claiming to be doing it for the
glory of the Lord. We even claim it as God's will when all

the while, faith is absent. Why? Because if we can do it on our own, it takes no faith at all! Everything we do in life is directly linked to our faith in the one true King. James said the same thing when talking about prayer. He said that if we don't pray with the faith that God will answer our prayers, then we are unstable in all of our ways (James 1:6–8). They are useless.

Sounds like there are a lot of powerless lives, homes, and churches in this nation, aren't there? Do you attend a local church for worship on a regular basis? Do you go because it is what Christians do? Or do you go because you expect to meet God there, and you know that He is going to move in a mighty way? Christians must be aware when our traditions and disciplines become routine. Because if we don't walk in faith, then we will begin to leave God out of our decisions, our worship, and His church. Many times, the things we do become faithless. They become just another thing we check off our daily checklist instead of an act of worship that requires pouring our hearts out to the Almighty for who He is and all He has done.

Second, we must remember that we "have been saved through faith." Due to that fact, everything in our life relies on the understanding that we are saved by grace through faith. Paul's point is that salvation comes through faith, and we can't gain it on our own because it is a gift from God.

Faith doesn't simply mean to believe something mentally, but instead you stake your life on it. Faith is an utter reliance and trust in and on Jesus Christ as the answer to every need in life. This is why it is impossible to boast about faith because the very nature of faith is in surrendering our own power and our own abilities to the Lord. It is saying, "I give up. Here, Jesus, You do it. I can't." In tying these two verses together, we find that it is impossible to please God without faith. In fact, it is useless and powerless. Why? We are saved by grace through faith, and God planned life in such a way that we would never boast or rest in our own merit.

We are His workmanship! We were created in Christ Jesus. He is the master architect. It boils to this: without faith, it is impossible to please God, and without Jesus, it is impossible to have faith. Listen, we can't leave Jesus out of a life where faith is required. Faith isn't something we do or have on our own, but something He produces in and through us as we surrender and live out His plans for our life.

Faith is not just believing in Jesus, but trusting Him with every single aspect of our life. It is surrendering to His will when we want our way. It's trusting Him to deliver us when in our own eyes, our situation looks useless. God laid out the entire plan beforehand, and He requires us to walk in them. Not based on our own power, lest we should boast, but by His power. "Lord, help me stop trying to change Your plans based on what I think or see, but help me to place my Faiths wholeheartedly in Thee!"

Thank you, Lord, that faith isn't left up to me to live out on my own, but help me to always realize that faith is found in my willingness to surrender to You and Your plan. Help me surrender today! Amen!

Faith Conquers Fear

There is no doubt that we need a fear-conquering faith. This type of faith is demonstrated throughout God's Word. This is the same faith demonstrated as Job kept the faith despite the trials, troubles, and persecutions. It is the same type of faith Daniel had in the lion's den. That Shadrach, Meshach, and Abednego had in the furnace. It is the same faith that kept Stephen preaching as he was stoned. It is the same faith that kept the apostles going as they experienced loss and adversity. It is a faith that stands firm when adversity strikes, claiming, "For God has not given us a spirit of fear and timidity, but of power, love, and self-discipline" (2 Tim. 1:7).

Anna and Andy's Story (Cayden's Story)

It is the same faith that God gave Anna that morning in November. Anna tells her story this way.

That morning as my kids and I awoke, we decided to put up our Christmas tree. As we were doing so, my husband Andy called and told me that the flower shop had a delivery for us. So I got dressed so that I could go pick up the delivery. My oldest son, Cayden, who was six at the time, was so happy to help me carry the pieces to our Christmas tree into the living room. A few minutes later, my dad called and asked if Cayden wanted to go fishing with him. Cayden loved to fish, and so I enthusiastically told my dad yes. I seized a moment of Cayden's excitement to inform him that if he wanted to go fishing with his Papa, then he must clean his room first. So Cayden cleaned his room, but asked me to make his bed as he was in a hurry to leave. I then laughed and agreed to make his bed. It was a great morning. I then helped dress Cayden for the fishing trip. He was dressed in his Alabama hoodie and the bracelet that I had given him the night before. This was funny because the bracelet was rolled up in the sleeve of his hoodie, so I had to dig around to get it out.

A little while later as we were now decorating the Christmas tree, my dad arrived to pick Cayden up for their fishing trip. I gave him a big hug, and they were off. I went about the next few hours cleaning and playing with my other two kids, Brady and Grayson. All of a sudden, the joy of the day was broken with one phone call. I remember the time as if it were yesterday. It was 11:30 a.m. The call came from my mother, and she was frantic. All I could hear was her wailing, screaming, and crying. It was to such an extreme that I could not understand what she was saying. I thought that something had happened to my grandfather or something. So I put the kids in the car and raced to her house. I remember telling the kids to sit still in the car while I ran it to see what was going on.

As I made it inside, she was still frantic, and I could not understand anything that she was saying, when all of a sudden, it hit me like a ton of bricks, and the words that she kept repeating took my breath away. She was screaming, "Your dad and Cayden had a boat wreck!" Needless to say, I was in shock. I did not know where they were, if they were injured, how badly they were injured, or how to find out. All I knew was that I had to hold it together for both of us so that we could find out.

My mom then informed me that they had called her off someone else's phone. So I immediately called back the same number that had called her, and a lady answered. The lady advised me that the accident was really bad and that they were loading them into an ambulance. I then asked the question that no mom wants to ask: "Is Cayden alive?" The lady then informed me that they were both breathing, but it did not look good. She further explained that a life-flight was meeting Cayden at the hospital in Camden, Alabama.

I then immediately left my mom and advised her to pull herself together, and I would be right back! I then took Brady and Grayson to Nana's house. I told them about the wreck, picked up my mom, and headed for Camden. On the way to Camden, I called my husband Andy to inform him about the wreck and had him meet us in Camden.

Needless to say, the ride to Camden was a blur. My mom was crying so hard all the way to Camden that she made herself sick. All the while, I was attempting to maintain my composure so that I could get to my child safely.

As we arrived at the hospital, I could see that the helicopter was ready to take off, but Cayden was still in the ambulance. I directed my mom to go check on my dad while I went to check on Cayden. I arrived at the ambulance only to find out that the paramedics would not let me see Cayden. So I immediately feared the worst! My fear was that he was so badly cut up that they did not want me to see him. All of a sudden, I noticed that the helicopter shut down its engine. My heart immediately sank a little deeper in my chest. Moments later, one of the paramedics delivered the news that I never thought that I as a mother would hear. Cayden did not make it. The paramedic told me that there was just too much damage to his brain. About that time, I saw my mom making her way to me, realizing that the news that I had just received was not good.

We were then escorted to a little meeting room by this nice lady. As we were on our way, I could hear a paramedic screaming, "He's breathing! He's breathing! He opened his eyes, and he is breathing!" And almost immediately, the helicopter restarted its engine and prepared for takeoff. They said that they were taking Cayden to Birmingham but ended up taking him to Montgomery. At that moment, I left my mom to take care of my dad as Andy and I headed to Montgomery.

The trip to Montgomery seemed to be one of the longest trips that I had ever taken, but I held on to hope, and I held on to my Bible. At that point, I still had no idea how my dad was or what was the extent of his injuries. All I knew was that Cayden was in bad shape, and I needed to get to him. En route to the hospital in Montgomery, we got lost twice, and the tensions were rising between me and Andy! We could both feel time slipping away. Not to mention the fact that our phones were blowing up as the news of the accident hit home. All that I could think about all the way to Montgomery was how blessed I was to be Cayden's mom. He was an amazing boy, and anyone would be privileged to be his mom.

When we arrived at the hospital, the process just to get in was frustrating, but once we got in, an attendant asked who we were and took us straight to a room that was set up to conference with families.

Many of our friends and family were already in the room waiting for us.

Almost immediately, when the doctor found out that we were there, they came into the room to meet with us. All that the doctor could do was shake his head. Finally he said that the damage was just too great and that Cayden did not make it. He then promised us that they had done all that they could. Needless to say, I was devastated! Nevertheless, I knew that they Lord was holding my hand, so I knew not to question Him. I remember repeating to myself, *I will not question My God!*

The whole room was filled with tears. Everyone was in total shock at the news that they had just heard.

Andy asked the doctors if he could see Cayden. I remember thinking, *I can't see him*. At this point, I was afraid that he was too beat up and cut up for me to handle seeing. I just couldn't handle seeing my baby like that. I remember asking my cousin Nikki to go and take pictures in case I was ever ready to see them. We were going to donate his organs, but we were too late to do so. We were only able to donate the cornea of his eyes.

As they returned after seeing Cayden, I asked Nikki if his face was too badly messed up. She assured me that it wasn't. So I worked up the nerve to see his picture, and he did look normal. So I then made the bold step to go see Cayden, and I am so glad that I did.

Needless to say, Andy was shocked to see me enter the room. I then sat beside Cayden and began to talk to him and hold his hand. I told him that I loved him and would miss him. I then touched his hand to my face on last time. I could feel the warmth of his body. I then told him to watch over us and that I knew he was going to be in heaven and that everything was okay.

I just sat there for a while, rubbing his hands and face. As I did, the room was immediately filled with a peace that surpasses all understanding. It felt like the Holy Spirit was right there, comforting us. It was strange and yet so comforting. I then kissed Cayden's head, told him that I loved him, and left the room.

We were filled with so many emotions. We were certainly glad to have so many who loved us there to support us. There is no doubt that we need one another in times of crisis. When we arrived back to Andy's truck to leave, we found a cross made of soft ties that Cayden had made on the step of Andy's truck. Immediately, there was another sense of peace that surrounded us.

Nevertheless, the ride back home was very difficult. I wanted to go be with my dad, but Andy and I were so physically and mentally drained that we thought it best to go home and get some rest.

I remember how encouraging message after message were on Facebook. Everyone shared their prayers, sent friend requests, messages, and even changed their profile picture to Cayden's picture. The support was almost overwhelming. Our pastor, Brother Mitch, was there whenever we needed him. As we arrived home, people wanted to come by, but we asked them to wait as we were extremely tired.

The next morning, Eddie and Martha came over to watch the boys so that we could go check on my dad. It was going to be bad facing my dad the first time since this tragedy. It was a long trip to Tuscaloosa, where they had taken my dad. I had no idea what to expect when we saw my dad. The final walk down the long hall to his room was one of the most difficult walks that I ever had to take, but a peace beyond all understanding seemed to be all around me.

Immediately when we saw my dad, he started crying. He just kept saying over and over, "Baby, I am so sorry. You know that I would never do anything to hurt that baby, don't you?"

I knelt beside his hospital bed and said, "Daddy, I know that you would never do anything to hurt my baby, and I don't blame you for what happened."

By that time, the whole room was in tears. Nevertheless, I knew that I had to hold it together because my mom and dad needed to see that despite this tragedy, my faith was wholeheartedly in God. I needed them to know that even though this had happened, my faith did no waver and was not shaken. I knew that God was on my side.

My dad then looked at me and began to tell me about the conversation that he and Cayden had on the way to fish. Cayden's Nana Nall had just gone to be with the Lord a short time before the incident. So that morning of the fishing trip, Cayden was telling my dad that his Nana Nall was with Jesus and went on to tell my dad that Jesus sometimes takes little kids too. At that moment, I fell apart. Little did I know that conversation would comfort me, but it would change my dad's life.

The following day, we made arrangements with the local funeral home. Once again, Andy and I were faced with another difficult task, but the peace of God surrounded us. So many times I asked myself, *How am making it?* but then God would make it clear that he was carrying me. God even placed people in our lives to help take care of the cost of the funeral. There is no doubt that "all thing were working out for our good and God's glory" (Rom. 8:28).

The Friday morning before the funeral, when I awoke, God spoke to me, leading me to ensure that the funeral was structured in such a way that there was an open invitation. I cried as I shared with Andy what the Lord was leading me to do because I was not sure we had the strength to do it. Again, God's peace consumed us, and he reassured us that He would be holding my hand, and that His is the only strength that we would need. I immediately called our pastor. He was in shock, but agreed. You see, God was really at work in my life like nothing that I have ever experienced before.

The day of the funeral it was raining really hard, but these drops of rain would pale in comparison to the tears that would be expressed in our local church on this day. I remember thinking about how beautiful everything looked. Flowers were everywhere. After the family's "so long for now" visit with Cayden's body drew to an end, an almost eternal line formed with friends, family, and loved ones. God had told me to speak, and I did right after my cousin and right before my pastor. The music, message, and the power and presence of God were amazing. There were many, many decisions for Christ that day as the invitation drew to a close, and among those making decisions were my dad, my brother, and my nephew. It was simply amazing how something so horrible like losing a child could result in so many lives saved. It was simply overwhelming to see my family eternally changed, all because of my sweet Cayden. I had never experienced God like that before in my life. I can honestly say that I have never felt so blessed or loved as I did on that day.

There is little doubt that each day is a little different than before, and each day brings with it its own challenges. God has truly taught us what it means to walk by faith and not by sight. There is no doubt that the prayers and support of our church, friends, and family have helped through this time of uncertainty, but it was because we continued to walk, trust, and rest in the power and presence of God. God had indeed given me a fear-conquering faith.

Day 31

Faith Leads to a Life of Prayer

Then the men set out from there, and they looked
down toward Sodom. And Abraham went with
them to set them on their way. The Lord said,
"Shall I hide from Abraham what I am about to
do."

—Genesis 18:16–17 (ESV)

We will continue learning to walk by faith by reading
the sixteenth verse of chapter 18 where these three visitors
(who came out of the hot desert into Abraham's tent and
who were unknown to him at first) now go their way to
accomplish the destruction of Sodom and Gomorrah.
Archaeologists are now convinced that it is the remnants of
the ancient cities of wickedness—Sodom and Gomorrah—
that have been rediscovered lying under the waters of the
Dead Sea. Our next chapter takes up the amazing historical
event of their destruction, but now we are looking at the
preview of it.

As Abraham's visitors leave his tent and go on their
way eastward to the valley of the Jordan, Abraham goes
with them. They come to a promontory at the edge of a
steep ravine, which leads down to the Dead Sea where
they can see the doomed cities lying far below them in
the afternoon sun. Tradition still marks the spot where
Abraham intervened with God for the city of Sodom.

As we look at this section of Scripture, we can learn some valuable lessons on the nature of prayer. First, we see that prayer begins with the proposal of God:

> The Lord said, "Shall I hide from Abraham what I am about to do, seeing that Abraham shall become a great and mighty nation, and all the nations of the earth shall bless themselves by him? No, for I have chosen him, that he may charge his children and his household after him to keep the way of the Lord by doing righteousness and justice; so that the Lord may bring to Abraham what he has promised him." Then the Lord said, "Because the outcry against Sodom and Gomorrah is great and their sin is very grave, I will go down to see whether they have done altogether according to the outcry which has come to me; and if not, I will know. (Gen. 18:17–21, RSV)

This marks a very important fact concerning prayer: prayer never begins with man; it begins with God! True prayer is never a man's plans, which he brings to God for him to bless. God is always the one who proposes. Prayer enters when God then enlists the partnership of man in carrying out his program. In other words, unless we base our prayers on a promise or a warning or a conviction of God's will, we have no right to pray.

Some people feel that the prayer of faith is crawling out on a limb and then begging God to keep someone from sawing it off, but that is not real prayer; that is presumption.

If God makes it clear that he wants us out on a limb, fine—we will be perfectly safe there. If not, it is presumptuous of us to crawl out on a limb, expecting God to keep us there.

The difference is simply this: the prayer of faith is acting on a previous knowledge of what God wants. It is always founded upon a promise. It begins with a proposal that God makes, or a conviction he gives, or a warning he utters. On the other hand, the prayer of presumption is discovering something we would like to do, and then asking God to bless it. That kind of thing is doomed at the outset. In fact, this is why so many "works of faith" fail, when they otherwise might have been wonderfully blessed of God.

Now when God proposes something, as he does in proposing to destroy the cities of Sodom and Gomorrah, he always enlists a man as his partner. So we have a picture of God talking to himself. He says, "Shall I hide from Abraham the thing I am about to do?" and he begins to list to himself the reasons why he should include Abraham in his plan. The reasons God lists might be called the rights of friendship. Here is where Abraham earned the title that is given to him in both the Old and the New Testament, "the friend of God" (2 Chron. 20:7, Isa. 41:8, James 2:23).

God says, "I won't keep this from Abraham for two reasons: first, because he has been given by grace a favored position in my sight. He is the man whom I have called out to become great. Through him all the nations of the earth shall be blessed. And second, I have chosen him in order that he might charge his household to keep the way of the Lord by carrying out righteousness and justice. I came into his life to show him how to do this, and because he has been taught by grace how to walk before God, this is the man to whom I want to tell my secrets."

Do you see the parallel of the Christian today? Every believer in Jesus Christ stands in exactly the same relationship with God. We have been given, by grace (not on our own merits), a favored position before God. We have been called into the family of God and made sons of the living God by faith in Jesus Christ. Furthermore, we are being taught by grace how to walk righteously before him, and as we learn that lesson, we become the people to whom God tells his secrets.

It is not enough to have the favored position. I think many Christians believe that because they have accepted Jesus Christ, all God has is now open to them. But there must be the walk, the daily appropriation of what he is, so that we learn to walk in righteousness. When we do, then God begins to share his secrets. I think the reason some people get a lot more out of the Bible than others is that they have learned this two-way relationship: God loves to tell secrets to his people.

> Lord, please help me to be faithfully dedicated to a life of prayer. May I never get too busy that I fail to ask for Your opinion, Your direction, Your provision, and Your Spirit to guide me.

Day 32

Faith Leads to a Life of Prayer (Continued)

God's proposal not only enlists the partnership of man, but is also based on an impartial and careful justice. The Lord says to Abraham in (Genesis 18:20), "Because the outcry against Sodom and Gomorrah is great and their sin is very grave, I will go down to see whether they have done altogether according to the outcry which has come to me."

This, of course, is the language of accommodation. God does not need to go down and visit any city in order to see what is going on. He is using Abraham's own language to express the truth, which reflects his nature. He talks as though a great outcry has been coming up to his throne from these wicked cities.

When I read this, I can't help but think that every sin of man is like a voice crying out from earth to heaven. What kind of a cry must be going up from America today as a result of the terrible flood of pornography inundating our theater programs and our literature and the tide of immorality that is sweeping across this country. God, according to this record, sees it all. God is walking in our streets and taking note of all that happens to us. He visits our homes and marks everything, missing nothing. He invades our most sacred privacy. Even our thoughts and subconscious ideas are naked and open before him.

Before he judges the cities of the plain, God carefully investigates the charges and probes to see what the conditions are. Then he tells Abraham that he is going to destroy these cities. Actually, he does not specifically tell Abraham what he will do, but when Abraham hears the ominous words "I will know," then he knows what God will do. Abraham knows all the unbridled lust, the foul acts of homosexuality, and the open passion for obscenity, the lurid and salacious attitude that permeated all public and private life in these cities. Abraham knows that the cities' doom is sure.

This agrees fully with what we read in the New Testament about prayer. In Romans, Paul says, "We do not know what we ought to pray for" (Rom. 8:26b). Do you know what to pray for about yourself or anyone else? No, you do not. But, he says, the Spirit himself intercedes for us with groans that words cannot express. And he who searches our hearts knows the mind of the Spirit (Rom. 8:26c–27).

Admittedly, in talking about prayer, we are treading at the edge of mystery, but through the mists, certain things are clear from this account of Abraham's prayer. Prayer makes possible, first of all, the joy of partnership. Did you ever see a little boy come into the house and say to his mother, "I'm going to help Daddy"? He is filled with pride about it, and he goes out and passes up nails and holds the boards and pounds his fingers. Daddy could have done the job better by himself, but he loves to have his son help him. And the son loves it too. There is a sense of partnership there. This is what prayer does. Through true prayer, God never moves entirely on His own. He loves to gather us in and have us help pound the nails. If we pound our fingers a little bit, He is there to soothe us.

Prayer also enables us to appropriate the character of God. Abraham is never more like God than at the moment he is praying for Sodom. His prayer did not save the city, and it was never intended to do so, but it did make Abraham manifest in his own life the mercy and the compassion of God. This is why God asks us to pray, that we might take upon ourselves something of His own character.

The third consideration: prayer focuses the power of God on an individual place or person. Although Abraham had never mentioned Lot by name, God remembered Abraham and saved Lot (19:29).

I don't know why prayer makes such a difference, but I know it does. We can plan a program, think through all the details, set up all the committees, get all the things we need, instruct everybody, and rehearse it, and at the final presentation, it may fall totally flat. But if we involve others in the ministry of prayer concerning the program, though the preparations may be similar, the difference in the presentation is that it comes with power, with impact, and with full strength, and lives are changed.

Lord, help us to be faithful in prayer. Help us to pray expectantly without ceasing. Lord, help us to realize that you want to give us abundantly and exceedingly more than we could ever ask. Amen.

Day 33

Maintaining a Fear-Conquering Faith

Abram believed the LORD,
and he credited it to him as righteousness.

—Genesis 15:6

Wouldn't it be awesome to maintain a faith that literally tears our fears apart? That is exactly the type of faith God want us to have. Abraham believed God and lived that way. Sure, Abraham was known as one of the mighty men of faith, but it isn't Abraham who was mighty. Is it that mind-boggling for us to believe God is who He says He is and that He will do what He says He will do despite the detriment and circumstances that hold us back? We get so trapped into thinking if only we had faith like Abraham or any other of the faithful, so often we compare our faith with theirs, but what a tragedy to focus on their faith. Don't we serve the same mighty God? Though it is true that Abraham's faith was credited to him as righteousness. It was not based on Abraham's righteousness, but instead, God's ability to deliver all that He promised. It was just credited to Abraham as righteousness.

You see, what made Abraham a man of great faith was that he wasn't focused on the difficulties of this world, but instead he kept his eyes on the Faithful One. The point is that Abraham realized the greatness of God! He realized that it makes no difference how big the problem is; God is greater! It doesn't matter how strong the opposition is; Our God is stronger! It doesn't matter how enormous the giant looks or how immovable the mountain seems; our God is all-powerful! Abraham credited his righteousness because he trusted God, and then in response to God's commands, he put his faith into action.

Not only did Abraham believe in the strength of God to overcome his fears, but he trusted God to deliver him from his fears. In other words, Abraham knew that God would always do as he promised. God credits righteousness to those who believe. Abraham believed that God would make his seed more numerous than the dust of the earth, and God credited it righteousness. What a beautiful truth! Abraham was not saved by good works, but rather, he believed God and was saved by Christ's righteousness. Jesus's perfection was stamped on Abraham's record in heaven. God the Father viewed Abraham from that point through the righteousness of our Savior.

Listen closely: Abraham believed God concerning the coming Messiah and His redemption. "And he believed in the LORD; and he counted it to him for righteousness" (Gen. 15:6). Why did God place merit as Abraham acted in faith? As we mentioned earlier, Abraham could not please God in his own merit or righteousness (Titus 3:5). It does not matter how much good we do; our sins are still recorded in heaven and must be dealt with according to

God's standards. That is why the Lamb of God came to earth and paid the price with His own precious blood.

Even in our sincerest efforts, we are tarnished with the curse of sin and rebellion. But because we are covered by the blood of His Son, we are credited righteousness. We are saved by Jesus's righteousness through faith. So as we deny ourselves, take up our cross daily, and follow Him, no matter what comes our way, He maintains within us a fear-conquering faith!

> Lord, would You please establish and maintain within us a fear-conquering faith! Amen.

Day 34

Trusting the Master's Hand

By faith Isaac invoked future blessings on Jacob
and Esau. By faith Jacob, when dying, blessed each
of the sons of Joseph, bowing in worship over the
head of his staff. By faith Joseph, at the end of his
life, made mention of the exodus of the Israelites
and gave directions concerning his bones.

—Hebrews 11:20–22

Before the portrait of our faith is drawn with our lives, we must have faith. As the portrait of faith takes its place in our hearts and our minds, our faith in Jesus becomes the foundation of our relationship with God. This faith is a surety that does not rest on logical proof or material evidence, but is instead the understanding that God did everything described in His word and will do everything He promised.

Faith is not something we have, as much as we live. Biblical faith believes that when God tells us something, it is done, and we can take it to the bank. No matter whether or not we can see it happen or see how it will happen, we believe. Faith means that we keep our eyes on God, who controls all circumstances, and not on the circumstances themselves.

God laid out all the details of our faith before we were even formed. We realize that as we unveil the truth that faith always gives God what is right, demands a life that is pleasing to God, a reverent fear of the Lord, is always willing to trust and obey, always yearns for home, is always willing to wait, and is always willing to sacrifice. Verse 6 says without faith, it is impossible to please him, for whoever would draw near to God must believe that he exists and that he rewards those who seek him.

We are going to look at how the Master's hand sketches out our life. To see that clearly, we must understand that faith is about the future, not the past. People of faith look into the future, they live for the future, and they plan and prepare for the future. In other words, all that we do is in preparation for that day! Faith is not about hiking back to some bygone time, but believing God for what he has promised.

It is natural as we get older to reflect back to "the good ole days" with fondness. But beware because much of what we are seeing is with rose-tinted glasses. If we are living in the past, we can't move to the future. And if we think about it, the toggle switch on the TV isn't quite as good as the remote. It wasn't that the times were so much better, just different. As we look at the lives of Isaac, Jacob, and Joseph, we will see the kind of attitude of faith as it looks toward the future. People of faith influence the future.

Faith is the pen that sketches the future (verse 20). Faith reaches into the future and shapes it. The inclusion of Isaac is interesting, since he accidently blessed Jacob. The truth is that he was deceived! Isaac knew in his heart that God wanted Jacob to have the blessing (read Genesis 25:23) even though Isaac favored Esau. When he was deceived and Esau said, "Do you only have one blessing?" he made no attempt to revoke the blessing but told Esau "Tough luck!" I think it was at this point that Isaac realized that he had been struggling against God and lost.

We can resist God and struggle against Him all we want, but He will win! But the blessings Jacob bestowed on his sons were an act of faith. He was allowing God's hand to reach into the future to shape it, and Jacob's faith in tune with God sketched His children's future by passing the blessing on.

Listen, that is what faith does. Faith is about the future, not the past. Isaac was not living in the past, harking back to the days of his father, but looking forward, believing that God had prepared the future of his sons and their sons, and that the promises of God would be greater than his. People of faith trust the hand of God as they sketch the future. As we do so, when things go wrong, we trust God to overrule and use our faith according to His plans (Jer. 29:11). By faith, we can make an impact on the future. It may be through our example, through our service, through our vision, through our praying, giving, etc., that others come to know the Lord.

There was a twenty-four-year-old farmer named Albert, who was a new Christian and enthusiastic for the Lord. He would fill his truck with people and take them church to hear about Jesus twice a week. There was young farmer's son who he always wanted to go with him, but he couldn't ever persuade him because he was too busy chasing the girls. Eventually, Albert was able to persuade him by asking him to drive the truck, and he did. Albert's guest went into the meeting and was spellbound. He went back night after night until he gave his life to Christ. It was 1934, and the young man Albert carried to church was Billy Graham. Albert didn't know that Billy Graham would speak to more people about Jesus than any other in history. But by faith, he sketched the future.

Faith is the paint that colors the blessings for the next generation (verse 21). By an act of faith, Jacob on his deathbed blessed each of Joseph's sons with God's blessing, not his own—as he bowed worshipfully upon his staff (verse 21). Jacob was seeking to pass on the blessing of God to the next generation. We cannot be held responsible for what the next generation does with it, but we are responsible for passing on the promises and blessings of God. We are responsible for seeking to share our faith with them.

People of faith want to bless the next generation, not condemn them. We want to pass on the baton. God has called us to make a difference for Him in our generation, but we mustn't just look to today; we must look to the next generation. What are we passing on to them? Do not underestimate your role as parents. There is a trend in society for more and more power and responsibility being taken from parents and given to others. I believe this is dangerous. We must not let that happen in the church.

John Wesley said, "I learned more about Christianity from my mother than from all the theologians in England." What can you do for the next generation? How can you pass on the blessing of God to them? Live out a faithful life in front of them. Take time to teach them to cultivate their own walk with God. Expose them to positive Christian influences that show them that following God is not boring or for wimps.

Day 35

Trusting the Master's Hand (Continued)

Faith is the detail that prepares us for the future (verse 22). Looking ahead, not just living for the moment, is a characteristic of people of faith because faith is about the future, not just the present.

Building for tomorrow starts today. We need to future-proof the church. We must pass on a blessing that molds the church. In other words, we need to pass on a hope and a future! If we want the next generation to serve Him with all their heart, their soul, their mind, and their strength, then we must allow Him to ignite the fire and zeal within us and pass it on. We need to be a people of faith, a people who look to the future.

Too often, Christians are accused of being backward-thinking people instead of forward thinking. We should be the most forward thinking of all people. We must be anticipating and preparing for the future. Faith does that. What are you expecting to happen in the future? Are there things that God has promised to you, things you are expecting? Then perhaps we need to, in faith, make some preparations for that. But there is one thing that we are guaranteed—it is that Christ will return!

One day we will stand before God—faith prepares for that future—Jesus parables. What do you need to be doing in preparation for meeting God face-to-face? What adjustments do we need to make in our lives? What gifts/talents/opportunities do we need to utilize to make sure we are ready to stand before God?

Faith Surrenders to God's Design

God's design for every human being, the home, the family, and the church are perfect. When we fail to surrender to His design, then it is not long that we begin to see the consequential effects from this defiance. We can see this clearly in the world we live in today as morality appears to be at an all-time low.

God's design is perfect in every way. *It began with the design of man and woman*: "From the beginning...God made them male and female" (Mark 10:6). "So God created man in His own image; in the image of God He created him; male and female He created them (Genesis 1:27, ESV)."

Then God designed marriage.

> Then God blessed them, and God said to them, "Be fruitful and multiply." (Gen. 1:28)

The Lord God caused a deep sleep to fall on Adam, and he slept; and He took one of his ribs, and closed up the flesh in its place. Then the rib which the Lord God had taken from man He made into a woman, and He brought her to the man. And Adam said: This is now bone of my bones and flesh of my flesh; she shall be called Woman, because she was taken out of Man. (Gen. 2:21–23, cf. Lev. 18:22, Rom. 1:26–32, 1 Cor. 6:9–11, 1 Tim. 1:10, and Jude 1:7)

For this reason a man shall leave his father and mother. (Mark 10:7)

If anyone does not provide for his own, and especially for those of his household, he has denied the faith and is worse than an unbeliever. (1 Tim. 5:8)

And be joined to his wife. (Mark 10:7, quoting Gen. 2:24)

The two shall become one flesh; so then they are no longer two, but one flesh. (Mark 10:8)

Let the husband render to his wife the affection due her, and likewise also the wife to her husband. The wife does not have authority over her own body, but the husband does. And likewise the husband does not have authority over his own body, but the wife does. Do not deprive one another except with consent for a time, that you may give yourselves to fasting and prayer; and come together again so that Satan does not tempt you because of your lack of self-control. (1 Cor. 7:3–5)

Marriage is honorable among all, and the bed undefiled; but fornicators and adulterers God will judge. (Hebrews 13:4)

Who can find a faithful man? The righteous man walks in his integrity; his children are blessed after him. (Prov. 20:6–7)

I will therefore that the younger women marry, bear children, guide the house, give none occasion to the adversary to speak reproachfully. (1 Tim. 5:14, KJV)

Admonish the young women to love their husbands, to love their children, to be discreet, chaste, homemakers, good, obedient to their own husbands, that the word of God may not be blasphemed. (Titus 2:4–5)

Submitting to one another in the fear of God. Wives, submit to your own husbands, as to the Lord. For the husband is head of the wife, as also Christ is head of the church; and He is the Savior of the body. Therefore, just as the church is subject to Christ, so let the wives be to their own husbands in everything. (Eph. 5:21–24)

Be submissive to your own husbands, that even if some do not obey the word, they, without a word, may be won by the conduct of their wives, when they observe your chaste conduct accompanied by fear. Do not let your adornment be merely outward—

arranging the hair, wearing gold, or putting on fine apparel—rather let it be the hidden person of the heart, with the incorruptible beauty of a gentle and quiet spirit, which is very precious in the sight of God. (1 Pet. 3:1–4)

Let the wife see that she respects her husband. (Eph. 5:33)

He who finds a wife finds a good thing, and obtains favor from the Lord. (Prov. 18:22)

Houses and riches are an inheritance from fathers, but a prudent wife is from the Lord. (Prov. 19:14)

Who can find a virtuous wife? For her worth is far above rubies. The heart of her husband safely trusts her; so he will have no lack of gain. She does him good and not evil all the days of her life. (Prov. 31:10–12)

Husbands, love your wives, just as Christ also loved the church and gave Himself for her....So husbands ought to love their own wives as their own bodies; he who loves his wife loves himself. For no one ever hated his own flesh, but nourishes and cherishes it, just as the Lord does the church....let each one of you in particular so love his own wife as himself. (Eph. 5:25, 28–29, 33)

Live joyfully with the wife whom you love. (Eccles. 9:9)

God then designed the family.

Children are a heritage from the Lord. (Ps. 127:3)

The fruit of the womb is a reward. Like arrows in the hand of a warrior, so are the children of one's youth. Happy is the man who has his quiver full of them. (Ps. 127:3–5)

Fathers, do not provoke your children to wrath; but bring them up in the training and admonition of the Lord. (Eph. 6:4)

Children, obey your parents in the Lord, for this is right. Honor your father and mother, which is the first commandment with promise. (Eph. 6:1–2)

Children, obey your parents in all things, for this is well pleasing to the Lord. (Col. 3:20)

Her children rise up and call her blessed. (Prov. 31:28)

Therefore what God has joined together, let not man separate. (Mark 10:9)

God then designed the church.

Upon this rock I will build my church; and the gates of hell shall not prevail against it. (Matt. 16:18)

We can see God's clear design for the church in Ephesians 1–3, but there is little doubt that the church would be built upon faith in Jesus Christ and the gospel message. Jesus is the head of the church as we serve as a body that remains faithful by "fearing God and keeping His commandments."

> He who keeps His commandments abides in Him, and He in him. (1 John 3:24)

> Unless the Lord builds the house, they labor in vain who build it. (Ps. 127:1)

> This is My commandment, that you love one another as I have loved you. (John 15:12)

God's design is perfect, and our walk of faith must be properly aligned to His design. We will see that as the Oliver family tells their story of faith.

The Oliver Family's Story

We grew up with a family who truly believed in the saying "A family that prays together, stays together." Our father was the anchor that held our family strong, strong in faith and unity. Our earliest memories are filled with our dad "doing for others." His main goal in life was to make sure each one of us made it to heaven. We never asked growing up if we were going to church. It was a given—*yes*. If the doors were open, we were there.

Everywhere we went, our dad shared his faith with friends and strangers. Our family seemed to be "untouchable"... until 2008. Our dad/hero was diagnosed with pancreatic cancer. Even now, writing those words takes our breath away. When devastation invades a fortress that was perfectly and purposefully built, it leaves you shocked and numb.

Our dad was a fighter. He wanted to show us that you fight for things worth fighting for, which was us, his family. He fought for three long/short years. He never blamed God or lost faith. He was in and out of so many hospitals and doctor's offices, but used that to share his faith. He used every opportunity to get to know doctors/nurses intimately (even if only knowing them for two days) to plead with them to come to church. He still led his small group at his home until just a few months before he died.

Our mom says our dad was a lot like King David, a man after God's own heart. Our dad sought God during good and bad times, but what sets him apart from other men is the fact that while other men hide from God during their sinful times, our dad still sought God's face.

We had many private talks during his sickness. During one of those times, we asked him if he was afraid to die. Our dad's reply was, "No, I am sad for y'all. I know you will mourn because I am gone, but it's a win-win for me." Our dad had always had an unwavering faith in God his savior. Therefore, it came as no surprise to us when he did not hold resentment toward God when the cancer came.

As time passed and the cancer remained, though others questioned and at times burned with anger about the unfairness, our dad continued with his peace. This was a peace he would hold with him until the very end.

His death was the darkest days of our lives. Still is. Our lives will never shine in the same way again. But thanks to our dad, he left us with a legacy of faith to carry on. We are amazed every day of the strength our family still carries. Is it any wonder though, looking back on his life, from when he was a young man writing love letters to his newborn daughters in the hospital begging them to live Godly lives, up to his final month still teaching young married couples and preaching to them Proverbs 16:3.

Dad believed in Proverbs 16:3 with his whole heart before his sickness, during his sickness, and at the end of his life. "Commit your actions to the Lord, and your plans will succeed."

As sad as we are to not have our dad to hold on this earth, we know his plans *did* succeed because he is embracing God in his new heavenly home. He left us with this strong legacy of faith to pass down to future generations. His faith is already touching his grandchildren, whom he never got to meet.

What we have taken from our dad's journey with cancer and eventually his death is to always walk in faith. Though our hearts ache with so much pain due to his loss, we have never once resented God for his passing. We cannot pick and choose when it suits us to stand with Him; God is good all the time. Thank you, Dad, for your amazing walk in faith.

Day 36

A Living Portrait of Faith

It was by faith that Moses' parents hid him for three months when he was born. They saw that God had given them an unusual child, and they were not afraid to disobey the king's command.

It was by faith that Moses, when he grew up, refused to be called the son of Pharaoh's daughter. He chose to share the oppression of God's people instead of enjoying the fleeting pleasures of sin. He thought it was better to suffer for the sake of Christ than to own the treasures of Egypt, for he was looking ahead to his great reward. It was by faith that Moses left the land of Egypt, not fearing the king's anger. He kept right on going because he kept his eyes on the one who is invisible. It was by faith that Moses commanded the people of Israel to keep the Passover and to sprinkle blood on the doorposts so that the angel of death would not kill their firstborn sons. It was by faith that the people of Israel went right through the Red Sea as though they were on dry ground. But when the Egyptians tried to follow, they were all drowned

—Hebrews 11:23–29 (NLT)

What does your picture of faith look like? I guess better yet, how does your portrait of faith look?

Larry King talks of three farmers that come together every day in a field during a horrible drought to hit their knees, look up to God, and pray that the skies will open up and give them the rain they need. Day after day they pray, but there seems to be no answer from God. So they become discouraged. Sure, they continue to meet every morning, but the discouragement shines through.

One morning, an uninvited stranger shows up at their prayer meeting and asks what they were doing.

They respond, "We're praying for rain."

The stranger looks at them and shakes his head and responds, "No, I don't think so."

The first farmer says, "Of course we're praying. We are down on our knees pleading for rain. Look around, see the drought. We haven't had rain in more than a year!"

The stranger just shakes his head and responds, "It will never work."

The second farmer jumps up and says, "This is all we know to do. We need the rain. Besides, we aren't asking only for ourselves, but for our families and livestock."

The stranger shakes his head as if he is not impressed. He responds again, "You're wasting your time."

The third farmer can't take any more, and in anger, he says, "Okay, Mr. Know-It-All, what would you do if you were in our shoes?"

The stranger asks, "You really want to know?"

"We wouldn't have asked, would we?"

The stranger said, "If you truly believed that God would answer your prayer, you would have brought an umbrella!"

Faith will be drawn using seven practical features.

1. *Faith always lives for God even when it is contrary to man's law (verse 23)*. Sometimes the laws of men may dictate disobedience to God (Exod. 1: 15–22). Moses's parents kept Moses alive by hiding him even though the law said to kill him. Daniel prayed to the Lord even though King Darius said anyone who prayed to another God would be thrown into a den of lions. Nebuchadnezzar made it a law to worship the golden image when the music was played, but three Hebrew boys refused to worship an idol. The Apostles preached the gospel even though the law forbade it. Today, it is politically incorrect to stand for biblical principles. What will you do? Obedience to God is a higher calling than obedience to the laws of men. Moses's parents feared God more than they feared Pharaoh. Do you? The Apostles stood for God even if it meant death.

> The high priest questioned them, saying, "We told you not to teach in this name, yet here you have filled Jerusalem with your teaching, and you intend to bring this man's blood

upon us." Peter and the apostles answered, "We must obey God rather than men. The God of our fathers raised Jesus, whom you killed and exalted Him at his right hand as Leader and Savior, to give repentance to Israel and forgiveness of sins. And we are His witnesses and so is the Holy Spirit, whom God has given to those who obey him." (Acts 5:27–32, ESV)

2. *Faith always lives for God by choosing the path of righteousness over the way of sin (verses 24–25).* We must not let this world define us (verse 24). Paul in his appeal to the Gentiles pleads for us by the mercies of God to present our bodies as a living sacrifice, holy and acceptable to God, which is your spiritual worship. He challenges us to no longer be conformed to this world, but be transformed by the renewal of your mind, that by testing you may discern what is the will of God, what is good and acceptable and perfect (Rom. 12:1–2, ESV). This world will attempt to mold us, but we must choose to be different. We are to zealously serve Him (Titus 2:14, 1 Pet. 2:9).

> It must be a way of life for us to reject sin and embrace righteousness (verse 25). It is true that sin will always bring immediate, temporary pleasure, but it will also bring permanent

heartache. Though righteousness may bring temporary hardship, it will bring permanent joy (2 Cor. 4:17).

Day 37

The Features of Faith

By faith, Abraham obeyed when he was called to go out to a place that he was to receive as an inheritance. And he went out, not knowing where he was going. By faith he went to live in the land of promise, as in a foreign land, living in tents with Isaac and Jacob, heirs with him of the same promise. For he was looking forward to the city that has foundations, whose designer and builder is God. By faith Sarah herself received power to conceive, even when she was past the age, since she considered him faithful who had promised. Therefore from one man, and him as good as dead, were born descendants as many as the stars of heaven and as many as the innumerable grains of sand by the seashore.

These all died in faith, not having received the things promised, but having seen them and greeted them from afar, and having acknowledged that they were strangers and exiles on the earth. For people who speak thus make it clear that they are seeking a homeland. If they had been thinking of that land from which they had gone out, they would have had opportunity to return. But as it is, they desire a better country, that is, a heavenly one. Therefore God is not ashamed to be called their God, for he has prepared for them a city.

By faith Abraham, when he was tested, offered up Isaac, and he who had received the promises was in the act of offering up his only son, of whom it was said, "Through Isaac shall your offspring be named." He considered that God was able even to raise him from the dead, from which, figuratively speaking, he did receive him back. (Hebrews 11:8-19, esv)

A man once prayed, "Lord, prop us up on our leaning side." After hearing him pray that prayer many times, someone asked him why he prayed that prayer so fervently. He answered, "Well, sir, you see, it's like this…I got an old barn out back. It's been there a long time, it's withstood a lot of weather, it's gone through a lot of storms, and it's stood for many years. It's still standing. But one day I noticed it was leaning to one side a bit. So I went and got some pine poles and propped it up on its leaning side so it wouldn't fall. Then I got to thinking about that and how much I was like that old barn. I've been around a long time. I've withstood a lot of life's storms. I've withstood a lot of bad weather in life, I've withstood a lot of hard times, and I'm still standing too. But I find myself leaning to one side from time to time, so I like to ask the Lord to prop us up on our leaning side 'cause I figure a lot of us get to leaning at times. Sometimes we get to leaning toward anger, leaning toward bitterness, leaning toward hatred, leaning toward cussing, leaning toward a lot of things that we shouldn't. So we need to pray, 'Lord, prop us up on our leaning side,' so we will stand straight and tall again to glorify the Lord. If you stare at this barn for a second, you will see who will help us stand straight and tall again."

> For we are God's masterpiece. He has created us
> anew in Christ Jesus, so we can do the good things
> he planned for us long ago. (Eph. 2:10, NLT)

The life of faith did not end for Abraham when he left Ur behind, nor when he finally set foot in the place God directed him. The story continues in verse 9. "Dwelling in tents" was the way of travelers and nomads. They were never considered permanent residences. The great lesson we glean from this part of Abraham's life is that as in our daily walk, true faith will always yearn for home. The problem is that we get so bogged down by our possessions and the places we have pitched our tent. We must remember that this world is not our home.

Abraham's faith went far beyond what he experienced in this life. His goal was a permanent, eternal home built by God. But make no mistake about it, "it is not metaphysical mirage that they are pursuing, for God has prepared for them a city, a real city, which, has real foundations" (verse 10). This is the homeland toward which the man of faith presses on. It is the same goal used as Christ urged his disciples to fix their gaze when, encouraging them to preserve in faith, he assured them that he was going to prepare a place for them and would come again to take them to be with him in this blissful abode (John 14:1–3). It is the same goal the apostle Paul, unhindered by present afflictions, pressed on, "forgetting what lies behind and straining forward to what lies ahead," in the conviction that our "citizenship is in heaven" where at last we shall be fully transformed into the likeness of our glorious Redeemer (Phil. 3:12, 20), and toward which we who are Christian believers hurry as we "run with perseverance the race that is set before us, looking to Jesus the pioneer and perfecter of our faith" (Heb. 12:1).

In such single-minded commitment, there can be no thought of turning back. The psalmist says,

> My soul longs, yes, faints for the courts of the LORD; my heart and flesh sing for joy to the living God. Even the sparrow finds a home, and the swallow a nest for herself, where she may lay her young, at your altars, O LORD of hosts, my King and my God. Blessed are those who dwell in your house, ever singing your praise! Selah. Blessed are those whose strength is in you, in whose heart are the highways to Zion. As they go through the Valley of Baca they make it a place offspring; the early rain also covers it with pools. They go from strength to strength; each one appears before God in Zion. O LORD God of hosts, hear my prayer; give ear, O God of Jacob! Selah. Behold our shield, O God; look on the face of your anointed! For a day in your courts is better than a thousand elsewhere. I would rather be a doorkeeper in the house of my God than dwell in the tents of wickedness. For the LORD God is a sun and shield; the LORD bestows favor and honor. No good thing does he withhold from those who walk

uprightly. O LORD of hosts, blessed is the one who trusts in you! (Ps. 84:2–12, ESV)

The descendants of Abraham also demonstrated this feature of their faith in verses 13–15. Verse 15 illustrates that the failure of the patriarchs to settle down in Canaan was not because their hearts were in Mesopotamia from where they came. They never returned to Ur even though they could have. Their hearts were yearning for home. Look at verse 16. The term *desire* means to "stretch out after" or "yearn after." They were unwilling to accept short-term satisfaction and instant gratification because that would deny them long-term fulfillment.

The verse says that God has "prepared for them a city" the word translated *prepared* (hetoimasen, Greek) is in the aorist tense (having been perfected). In other words, what is being done is perfect. The faith that they are demonstrating is demonstrated by two objects: a tent and an altar. With the tent they confessed their attitude toward this world; they would not let instant gratifications and eye-warming attractions blind them to spiritual realities. With the altar they confessed they were believers! Thus they adopted the attitude of a believer and lived as though they were strangers (away from home) and pilgrims (on their way home).

3. *Faith is always willing to wait (verses 11–17).* Abraham waited patiently for the promise. Often the hardest times for us as believers are the

in-between times. These are better known as times of waiting. Look at verses 11 and 12 as they testify to Sarah's faith. Do you ever feel like God has put your life on hold? That is what Abraham and Sarah must have felt like because for twenty-five years, they waited for the fulfillment of the promise. As time went on, they both passed the normal age of childbearing. Abraham knew God's promises, and realizing that nothing had occurred, he asked if perhaps his servant Eliezer was the one through whom the promise would be fulfilled (Gen. 15:2–3).

Waiting is one of life's greatest disciplines. Waiting time is never wasted time. What is God doing while you wait? He may be testing us to reveal how committed we really are. Regardless of how it appears, God is always working behind the scenes, preparing the way. God always uses life to position us and prepare us to accomplish His vision in our lives. We may be waiting because we are still about our agenda. Though we may have to wait, we must remember that God's timing is always perfect and right. True faith is always willing to wait for the fulfillment of God's promises in God's timing. We never lose when we trust God in the dark.

4. *Faith is always willing to sacrifice (verses 18–19).* The final feature of faith is the willingness to sacrifice (verses 17–19). It was by faith that Abraham offered

his son Isaac as a sacrifice when God tested him. Abraham demonstrated a willingness to give God the most important thing in his life, his son.

What is the most important thing in your life? God will never settle for being second place in your life. God is only interested in being first place in your life, and He will never settle for anything less.

Corrie ten Boom once commented that she had learned to hold the things of this world loosely in her hand because she knew that if she grasped them tightly, then the Lord would have to pry her fingers away, and it would hurt.

Is there anything in your life that you are trying to withhold from God? Is there anything that is going to hurt if God has to pry it out of your hands? Listen, we don't have any trouble sacrificing the unimportant things. For some of us, money is first place in life. You withhold what rightfully belongs to God. Remember the story of the rich young ruler (Matt. 19). This young man came to Jesus and asked what he must do to inherit eternal life. Jesus told him in verse 16 to "go and sell what he has and give it to the poor." *The point was not the money!* But Jesus knew that the money was where his heart was. It was first place in his life.

God is not interested in your money; he is interested in your heart. When Abraham was willing to give to God the most important thing in his life, God gave it right back to him. For some of you, the most important thing in your life is your family. For others, the most important thing in your life is your career, your dreams for the future. If you're afraid to trust God with your possessions, your dreams, or someone in your life, then you need to take a look at the life of Abraham. Because Abraham was willing to give up everything for God, he received back far more than he could even have imagined. True faith involves a willingness to sacrifice.

One crucial question demands an answer: if faith is so great, why do so few people live it? Well, most people would rather do anything than take a risk. Taking risks means being vulnerable. And that may affect our finances, our friends, our future, our feelings, our occupation, where we live, and a host of other considerations. The human tendency is to want to be safe and secure, to hedge our bets, to ensure ourselves against loss. Basically, we fail at faith because we fear to take the risk.

Day 38

A Faith Recognizes True Riches

5. *Faith lives for God and recognizes true riches (verse 26).* We must count things as they really are (verse 26a). The criticism that the world gives us is worth more than all the riches of this world. Real riches are those that are not of this world. We must recognize that the greatest riches are yet to come, so we fix our hearts on that reward.

The reward that is coming to those who follow Jesus outweighs anything this world can give. We must consider that the sufferings of this present time are not worth comparing with the glory that is to be revealed to us. Creation waits eagerly, longing for the revealing of the sons of God. Creation itself will be set free from its bondage to corruption and obtain the freedom of the glory of the children of God. For in this hope, we were saved. Now hope that is seen is not hope. When we hope for what we do not see, we wait for it with patience (Rom. 8:18–25, ESV).

6. *Faith always focuses on living for the living God (verse 27).* When we trust in God, we will not fear what men will do to us. Remember Moses, Peter, Paul, James, and John. Our focus must be on the One that the world does not see. How do we do that? We focus on him through staying in His Word (Ps. 119:11, 119:50). We draw our strength from Him through prayer (Ps. 138:3, Isa. 40:31). We see him through remembrance of His faithfulness (Ps. 143:5, 63:6).

7. *Faith always follows the path of victory (VV. 28-29).* What is the path of victory? The path of victory is the path of obedience (verse 28). We must obey even when obedience isn't appealing. Many times God's way goes against comfort. God commanded the Israelites to put blood on the doorposts and lintels of their houses. God's way does not appeal to the religious. The religious want to work for salvation. God's Way is by grace through faith (Eph. 2:8–9).

The path of victory is one that is saturated with God every step of the way (verse 29). As we see victory, we realize that only God could provide it. There is no way to accomplish God-sized tasks except in and with God. Real faith is alive and active. It never rests because it is always seeking God.

As the old pastor spoke, a young man was greatly moved. The preacher said, "When you have a religious impression, the time to act upon it is right then!" The time when you hear God's call is the exact time you should respond. So the young fellow walked down the aisle and made public his surrender to Jesus Christ, saying, "Preacher, it shall be right now that I take Jesus as my Savior."

The young man went back to the sawmill in the mountains where he worked, and he sang all morning as they moved the great logs to the sawmill. He claimed to them that this was the first morning that he had ever known such freedom. He loved what it felt like to be Christ's trusting disciple and follower.

Just before lunch, his body was caught somehow in the machinery and crushed and mangled, so that a little while thereafter, he went away into dusty death. When they got him out, he faintly said, "Send for the preacher, that preacher in the church at the foot of the mountains that I talked to last night."

The preacher fortunately was soon found and hurried up the mountain to the mill, and he bent down by the side of the dying fellow and took his hand and said, "Charley, I have come. What would you like to say?"

And with a smile on his face that was never on land or sea, he faintly pressed the minister's hand and said, "Wasn't it a glorious thing that I settled it in time?"

Oh, men and women, my men and women, I beg you, in the great Savior's name, turn your boat upstream before it is too late! "Now is the accepted time. Now is the day of salvation" (2 Cor. 6:2).

Day 39

A Perfected Faith

And all these, though commended through their
faith, did not receive what was promised, since
God had provided something better for us, that
apart from us they should not be made perfect.
Therefore, since we are surrounded by so great
a cloud of witnesses, let us also lay aside every
weight, and sin which clings so closely, and let
us run with endurance the race that is set before
us, looking to Jesus, the founder and perfecter of
our faith, who for the joy that was set before him
endured the cross, despising the shame, and is
seated at the right hand of the throne of God

—Hebrews 11:39–12:2 (esv)

Every person mentioned in Hebrews 11 received God's
approval because of their portrait of faith. They all looked
forward to God's promise, salvation, and a better day, but
not one of them received them all. Sure, they received some
of God's promises, but not the promises of the coming
Savior and His eternal Kingdom. Though they did not live
to see all His promises, their citizenship was secure in the
Kingdom of God. And they based their lives on what they
could not see.

Hebrews 11 has been called faith's "hall of fame." So
with that in mind, there is no doubt that the conclusion of

the chapter shocks many who read it. These mighty heroes of faith did not receive God's full reward because they died before the coming of the Savior. It is so clear that enduring hardship and testing are part of God's plan for those whose faith was of Old and New alike. It is also so very clear that God has far better things in mind for those who follow and trust Him. The far better things that God has in mind refer to the new covenant. Listen, those in the Hall of Faith did not receive this, but rather, we who came after the Lamb of God took our place experience it. Why? Because He paid a debt we could not pay, He conquered what we could not defeat, and He paved the way and ushered in His new promises. We share the prize with the heroes of old. Hear this today, not only are we one in the body of Christ with all those alive, but we are also one with all those who ever lived. One day the dead in Christ will rise, and together we will share in the promised blessing with Jesus. We will then be complete and perfect in Him.

Jesus is the author and the finisher of our faith. Let's skim through Hebrews 11 by talking about a passage that details a man who Jesus described as having the greatest faith ever seen.

Matthew 8:5–10 says,

> One day a Roman army officer came to Jesus and said, "I have a servant who's very ill. In fact, he's paralyzed and he's suffering in bed." Jesus said, "I'll

go to your house and heal him." And the Roman centurion said, "O Lord, You don't need to do that. I understand authority and I'm not worthy for You to come to my house. But I know this obedience and authority thing. I'm a captain in the army. I give commands to my soldiers and they obey immediately. I make commands to my servants and they obey me immediately. They do whatever I tell them to do. So I understand authority and obedience. You don't need to come to my house, Jesus. If You just say the word from right here I'm sure he'll be healed instantly." Jesus looked at that man and said, "This is the greatest faith I've ever seen in Israel."

What? How?

Faith and obedience can't be separated. They are permanently welded together. The truth is when we truly trust someone, we do what they say. If we don't, we don't trust them. God linked faith and obedience together in such a way that every promise of God is conditioned upon following the directions that He gives us. Deuteronomy 5:33 says, "Follow all the directions the Lord has given you. Then life will go well for you." That's a promise we can build our life and faith upon. God made some incredible promises in His word about obedience. The Bible says that if we follow God's directions, we will find joy. We will live longer. We will lack nothing good and will have all we need. And guess what? That's just a few. There are more than seven thousand promises in the Bible. Think about it, we could memorize a promise a week, and it would take us over twenty years to make it through them all.

What would your portrait of faith look like if you claimed them all? If you knew them, trusted them, and followed the directions, you would change the world! But for many of us, we won't because we have separated faith and obedience. I know some don't make sense to us in the flesh, but God says act upon them anyway. It's a matter of faith and a matter of obedience! Obedience is a demonstration of faith. It is a living and active faith. Obedience is the key that unlocks God's blessings. How many of us have either thrown the key away or misplaced it? As a pastor, I don't want anyone to miss out on all the promises. I don't want anyone to miss the fact that God will bless you, save you, watch over you, take care of you, help you, give you joy, a long life, you'll lack nothing, you'll have what you need, and you'll have a perfected faith. What must we do in order to unlock God's blessing?

We do four things, and He does the rest.

1. Obey God immediately!
    Don't wait. Don't procrastinate. Don't put it off. Don't make excuses. Don't drag your feet. Just do it. Right now. Not later. Now! Psalm 119:32 says, "I

will quickly obey Your commands…Without delay I hurry to obey Your commands."

If there's any time in life we really ought to hurry, it's when God tells us to do something. Don't delay; obey God immediately whether we feel like it or not, whether we understand it or not. Just do it immediately.

I feel I must say something that is so key here. We don't have to understand something to benefit from it. I don't understand how heavy planes fly, but I fly in them. I don't understand how computers work, but I use them. I don't understand internal combustion, but I'd rather drive than walk. Listen, we don't have to understand to receive the benefit. In the same way, we don't have to understand God's commands in order to obey them and receive His blessing. Every parent knows that when we tell a kid to do something, they'll say, "Why?" and you say, "Because I said so."

Listen, what we are actually saying is "Your little pea brain isn't big enough to understand it yet, but one day you will. But right now just trust me! At this point we know better than you, or this is for your own good, so you do it." This is what is meant by "Because I said so."

Listen close. God sometimes tells you to do something, and you say, "Why?" and He says, "Because

I said so. One day you're going to understand, but now, just do it." It is pretty bold to question the creator of the universe. But what if you don't have a good attitude? Obey anyway. Yes, I am saying obey God with a bad attitude. Absolutely. It's far better than disobedience. Parents shame on us for molding our kids to respond the opposite way. If you tell them, "I want you to this or that, but if you have a bad attitude, forget it." Guess what? They are never going to do it. What if God responded to our needs at the same speed that we obey Him? If we want the blessings of God, we must obey God immediately. If we want all the blessings of God in our life, we must also…

2. Obey Him completely!
   Not just immediately but completely. We don't say, "I'll take this one, but not that one… I like this command, but this one doesn't apply…" Listen, partially obedience is total disobedience. Psalm 119:4 says, "Lord, You gave Your orders to be obeyed completely."

   We must obey God completely. To do so, we must understand that *God's standard of right and wrong has never changed*. It never has, and it never will. If something was wrong six thousand years ago, it's still wrong today. If it was right back then, it is still right today. Lying was wrong for the children of Israel, and it is still wrong today. Truth doesn't change. Culture changes, popular opinion changes. Lots of things change, but truth does not change. And what's right is right, and what's wrong is wrong, regardless of what the popular opinion polls say.

God has a bigger perspective than us. He sees things we can't see. Us trying to see things from God's perspective would be like an ant trying to see things from your perspective. It isn't going to happen. You're not capable of seeing it all like God sees it all. We need to trust Him. James 4:11 says, "Your job is not to decide whether God's law is right or wrong, but to obey it." In 2 Kings, there is a story about a guy named Naaman. Naaman had leprosy. He went to Elisha and said, "I'm a very famous man, but I've got leprosy. What do I do?" Elisha said, "I'll tell you what. Just to show your faith, God wants you to go down to the Jordan River and dunk yourself under it seven times." Naaman says, "You've got to be kidding. It's humiliating." Elijah says, "Yes, it's humbling yourself before God." On the last time he comes up, he was cured of his leprosy. Was there special power in the water? No. It was because he was obedient to God. He had faith. And he obeyed God completely. Obey God immediately and completely.

3. Obey God joyfully!

   Psalm 100:2 says, "Obey Him gladly." Psalm 119:16 says, "I enjoy obeying Your commands." Psalm 119:47 says, "I find pleasure in obeying Your commands." How was it enjoyable to do what God tells you to do? It's enjoyable because I love God. I know what He's done for me, so I love Him, and I want to obey Him.

   In marriage, the longer you live together, the more you know what offends and grieves your spouse. Am I right? The longer you're married, the more you figure out what will offend that person. Like blowing your nose at the dinner table or passing gas on the couch or leaving the seat up on the toilet. You learn what offends your partner. But if you love that person, the longer you're married, the less you do those things because you don't want to offend them or hurt them. You love them.

   When you walk with the Lord through many years, the more you realize what God has done for you, how good He's been to you, the less you want to offend Him. You enjoy doing the right thing. You enjoy keeping His commands. You do it because you love God. Do you know how God measures your love? Not by what you say. ("I love You! I praise You!") God measures your love by your obedience. By how well you follow directions.

Jesus said, "If you love Me, keep My commandments." That's how we prove our love. If you want the blessings of God in your life, you obey Him immediately, completely, joyfully and…

4. Obey Him continually!

Life is not a fifty-yard dash. It's a marathon. God doesn't want you to just love Him some of the time. He doesn't want you to obey Him every once in a while or even most of the time, but every day of your life.

Psalm 119:112 says, "I am determined to obey You until I die." It says, "Lord, I will do what you say till I die." Have you made that choice?

Psalm 119:33 says, "Just tell me what to do and I'll do it, Lord. As long as I live I'll wholeheartedly obey." Just tell me what to do, and I'll do it. Would you make that your prayer today? Some of you are saying, "Why doesn't God tell me what to do? I've been praying what to do in this situation." I'll tell you why He hasn't told you. Because you're not already doing what He's already told you to do. Why would He give you more direction when you haven't acted on the truth He's already told you?

Philippians 3:16 says, "We must be sure to obey the truth we have learned already."

Day 40

A Faith That Always Endures

Consider him who endured from sinners such
hostility against himself, so that you may not grow
weary or fainthearted.

—Hebrews 12:3

The key to success in the Christian life is the same as it was for Christ and the heroes of our faith. Spiritual success is found in the ability to endure. In Hebrews 12:3, we read how we are to consider Christ who "endured such contradiction of sinners against himself, lest ye be wearied and faint in your minds."

If there is one character flaw that we should be without, it would be that we are quitters. A Christian should never quit. We are admonished over and over again to endure, to stay in the fight to the very end. Then as we look back at all the heroes mentioned in chapter 11, we note that they too were people who were able to endure to the end. Note what the Bible says about Moses (11:27), how he was a man of endurance.

Let's go back to the story of Moses and take a look at his life to see how he fought through great adversity, and at the ripe *young* age of eighty, God found a use for him.

What does an enduring faith look like?

Faith endures the past (Exodus 2:11–15). The early life of Moses was characterized by running away from things. Many people today spend their lives on the run, and like Moses, they are running from the past. Moses was on the run. He was a fugitive who was running from Pharaoh into the Midian Desert. He had made a mistake, and now he was running from it.

How many times have people shown up in churches who you later find out were running away from a problem in another place, another church, or another town? Anyone who does anything for God becomes a target of the devil. One of his favorite tools to use on people is to attack their character. Maybe it was earned, maybe not…

Faith keeps us from running from God. Many people are not just running from the past, they are running from God. The prophet Jonah could tell us how to do that. Just as Jonah learned, God knows where you are tonight, and He can find you, move you, and stop you anytime He pleases. You cannot hide from the eyes of God. "The eyes of the Lord are in every place beholding the evil and the good" (Prov. 15:3).

Too many believers are running in circles. Moses, like the children of Israel whom he would later lead, was running in circles. He was wandering in the Midian Desert tending sheep. Here he was, raised in the palace of Pharaoh as a son of Pharaoh's daughter, and he was out tending sheep. What an ending after such a prominent beginning to his life.

Moses was running in circles, lost and wondering. He was lost to himself, but he was not lost to God. He was far from the palace of Pharaoh, in a dead-end job herding sheep.

Many of you feel like you have made it as far as you can go in life. You have reached your limits, that this is your lot in life. But this is where God steps in and says, "Moses, Moses." He is talking to you tonight, calling your name, saying something like "Remember me?"

Are you wandering in the wilderness of life today?

Faith keeps us moving forward toward God (Exodus 3:1–4). At eighty years of age, Moses turned from his wanderings and turned to see God. You are never too old to get saved, never too old to serve God. Walking by faith will keep us from turning back (away from God). "And Jesus said unto him, No man, having put his hand to the plough, and looking back, is fit for the kingdom of God" (Luke 9:62).

It is time we decide to follow Jesus again, no turning back, no turning back. The prodigal son came to a place in his life when he realized how bad he wanted to go home to his father. It will keep us from turning to our circumstances. Moses used every excuse in the book:

1. Not fit (3:11)
2. No authority (3:13)
3. No power (4:1)
4. No eloquence (4:10)

What excuse have you been using on God? Faith will keep us returning to Christ, looking unto Jesus, the author and finisher of our faith (Heb. 12:2). Which way are you turning? Are you headed toward Jesus? Are your eyes fixed on Him? Or are your eyes cast upon the world and its pleasures?

Faith helps us return to Egypt (Exodus 4:18–20). Egypt for Moses was the place of God's service. God has a *place*, a location where He wants you to be at so you can serve Him. Now that Moses had turned to Christ, Egypt was where the racecourse was for him. Where has God laid out your racecourse? For now, it is right here at First Baptist Church. Right now, it is to the people who live next door to you. Right now, it is to the people you work with every day. Right now, it is to your husband, your wife, your children.

Hebrews 12:1 tells us that we are to run the race. God has called *every* Christian into His service. God did not save you just to occupy or hold the fort (parable of the talents); He saved you so that you can be one of His soldiers—a runner for Him. Get in the race!

Moses was a wanted man. He was wanted by Pharaoh for murder, and he was wanted by God for service. God knew where to find him. God equipped him. Some of us are on the back side of the desert as far as your Christian service is concerned. God is calling us to get back on course and back in the race. God wants you, wherever you are! God is calling you to walk by faith and not by sight.

References

Crossway Bibles. Study Bible, English Standard Version. 2007. Wheaton, Illinois: Crossway Bibles.

Holy Bible, King James Version. 1999. New York: American Bible Society. Bartleby.com, 2000. www.bartleby.com/108/.

Holy Bible, New International Version. 1978. Grand Rapids, Michigan: Zondervan.

Holy Bible, New Living Translation. 1996. Wheaton, Illinois: Tyndale House.

Nelson's Ultimate Bible Reference Library. 2008. Thomas Nelson, Inc.

CPSIA information can be obtained
at www.ICGtesting.com
Printed in the USA
FSOW01n1543010716
22267FS